DREAM ZONE

Dreams, Astral Travel, and Spirit Communications

Elaine M. Kuzmeskus, M.S.

ISBN: 978-1-59330-845-2

Printed in the United States of America

Table of Contents

Introduction:
"Fame Is On Your Horizon"

As a child I was always fascinated by the supernatural-- my favorite TV show was *The Twilight Zone.* Each week Rod Serling would introduce the program in his baritone voice: "There is a fifth dimension, beyond that which is known to man. It is a dimension as vast as space and as timeless as infinity. It is in the middle ground between light and shadow, between science and superstition."

We enter such a timeless dimension when we go to sleep each night. Here dreams can be as scary as a horror movie or as enlightening a vision of Mother Mary. With practice the dreamer can spend more time in the higher realms and even increase psychic abilities. While some dreams are precognitive, others shed light on past lives. Dreams can also be a source of after- life visitations and have the potential to heal grief.

I know because I have had usual contacts with the other side of life every since I was in my crib, in this dream zone. For instance, when I was about four, a Hindu gentleman only I could see taught me astral projection. My Hindu guide was giving me instructions: "Cross your fingers and place them over the middle of your forehead." As I did so, I saw what looked like a tunnel of dark light. " Now concentrate and push the energy forward." he continued. I did and soon I was able to see people and see them in their future state.

By the time I was seven I realized not everyone was psychic. Like most children, I did not share my knowledge of a spirit guide with those around me. However, I was fortunate to live in a family that was tolerant of the psychic. My Irish grandmother was really my first teacher. Nana would always say," Don't have to be afraid of the dead. It is the people who are alive that you have to fear." My grandfather was also interested in psychic matters. He loved to share unusual stories from the *Boston Herald'*. One evening he read aloud the article on the reincarnation of Bridey Murphy.

No wonder, by the time I was ten, I was having dreams of another life in the 1800s as a widow abandoned by her four sons. It seemed that we lived on a ranch outside of town. One morning as I was drawing water from the well, I had a heart attack. As my physical body fell backward, my spirit body separated and moved forward. "That's all there is to death", I thought, "you just drop your body."

As a child, I simply accepted guidance from dreams and my Hindu guide. By the time I entered college, I sometimes just ignored guidance much to my dismay. For example, when I heard "Use the other dryer" at the Kenmore Square laudromat. I stubbornly kept putting my wet clothes into the drier I had chosen along with all my change. When I turned the knob, the dryer did not turn on. Out of money, I had to carry a heavy load of wet wash back to my apartment!

However, about my junior year at University of Massachusetts in Boston, I began to study dreams in earnest. It all started when our Educational Psychology professor Dr. Halpern gave the students the choice of doing a dream journal for two weeks or a term paper. Naturally, I chose the former. It wasn't long before, realized that many of my dreams were psychic.

About the same time, I started reading books such *The Sleeping Prophet* and *The Autobiography_of a Yogi*. The "sleeping prophet" was the biography of Edgar Cayce who had died before I was born. Cayce seemed to be the only person I knew who also saw colors and spoke with dead people. He also explained the there were many spirits in the lower realms close to the earth. The task of the meditator was to rise above the sea of faces.

I tried daily candle meditation. Soon I was watching a crowd of spirits seeking to get my attention during the meditation. I ignored the sea of faces and sought a higher sphere. That's when I saw a man in a wheel chair who had lost both lower limbs and a woman who held out a purple flower. The female spirit said, "That's my name referring to the flower. Later I learned that my mother's grandfather, a year before his death had had lost his limbs to diabetes. His housekeeper's name was Violet.

Edgar Cayce's advice had been most helpful in contacting the other side of life. Apparently my tie with Edgar Cayce was a deep one. We were both drawn to ancient Egypt. In the Cayce readings, he had been told that he was the priest Ra-Ta who advised Nefertiti and Akhenaton. Later, in a vision, I saw myself as an Egyptian initiate, lying still in a huge sarcophagus. I knew then that it was my destiny. to be a medium.

Another gentleman who played a key role in my psychic development was Paramahansa Yogananda. He seemed to be looking over my shoulder as I read his book, *Autobiography of a Yogi.*. Trying to be true to his Yogi teachings, I put spiritual practices first and let material concerns slide. Predictably, it wasn't long before I was out of rent money. Soon, I began to pray in earnest for some work. The next morning, before I had even got out bed, I received a call from the Boston Public Schools asking me if I would like a job as a substitute. The call was quite a surprise, as I been on their list for months with no job offers.

Still I had never met a psychic until my first reading with Rev. William Ellis in July of 1969 at the First Spiritualist Camp of Etna, Maine. Rev. Ellis, a spry man in his sixties, explained, "You know there are seven planes and each plane has seven planes so there are forty-nine in all." His guide from the seventh plane told me my aura was yellow (my favorite color) and announced my present boyfriend and I were not getting along (true), and accurately described Nana who had died when I was ten. I was so impressed I went back two weeks later for another reading. This time Rev. Ellis ended the reading with, "Someday you will be doing this work. "No way", I thought. He immediately picked up my thought and added, "I know you don't believe me, but some day you will." We both laughed when I met Rev Ellis a third time when I was serving as a guest medium at Camp Temple Heights!

When I left Camp Etna, I took some Spiritualist literature with me. I immediately noticed that there was a development circle in Brookline, Massachusetts, where I was living at the time. Of course, I had to go. The person I met at the circle was Rev. .Kenneth Custance , a distinguished silver-haired medium I immediately trusted him-- something I do not usually do. Soon, I was a regular at the Friday circle hosted by his wife, Rev Gladys Custance, a trance medium.

They were a unique duo, for both were accomplished harpists, Spiritualist mediums, and ordained ministers. Always impeccably dressed, the two made a regal couple-- complete with spirit guides. While Kenneth had a Franciscan monk, 'the Abbot", Gladys had a Hindu guide, "the Professor" It was really Professor who conducted the development classes. His instruction on affirmations and meditation proved invaluable. Soon I was experiencing the most extraordinary meditation sessions.

I also took time to visit some of Boston's spiritual centers. Two come to mind--The Ladies Aide Society and the Home of Truth. The two groups had completely different settings. The former was a Spiritualist center in the basement of a run-down section of Boston, while the Home of Truth was housed in an elegant Boston mansion, donated for public service. Naturally each drew a different audience.

The Ladies Aide Society was run by medium Gertrude McCauley. Rev. McCauley ran a tight ship. If anyone dared to come into the afternoon service bogged down by shopping bags, the seventy year old medium would wag her finger and say "Don't you be visiting Mr. Jordan's or Mr. Filene's before you come to church." Her congregation would laugh at mention of Boston's popular stores.

While I admired Rev. McCauley, I was somewhat intimidated by her forthright manner. On several occasions she mentioned she saw "Connecticut" over my head. Meekly, I responded "I have never been to Connecticut, Rev. McCauley." Without missing a beat she replied, "You will be going soon." She was right. About a year later I married (a fact predicted by Rev. McCauley) and moved to Connecticut, where I have lived for past forty years.

I also enjoyed attending lectures at the Home of Truth in one of Boston's tonier neighborhoods. It was elegantly decorated-- its white walls trimmed with gold, Oriental rugs on the polished wood floors, and beautiful oil paintings throughout the mansion.. One of the most memorable speakers was English theosophist, Dr. Douglas Baker. Not only was he an excellent medium with the deceased poet Robert Browning as his spirit guide, and he was a medical doctor. I listened with rapt attention to the imposing gentleman twenty years my senior as Dr. Baker gave lectures on opening the third eye and astral travel. I even obtained a reading with him. As the medium/doctor concentrated on my aura, he accurately diagnosed a medical condition when he said "You suffer from anemia." He then advised trying radionics as a cure. Next, without any pause, he quickly scribbled observations the individual rays of each my seven bodies. By now, I was truly impressed. According to Dr. Baker, my soul was on the second ray of love-wisdom; my physical body was governed by the first way of will; and the mental body by the sixth ray of ceremonial magic. He also sensed that two older people would be very helpful with my spiritual studies. I immediately thought of Gladys and. Kenneth Custance.

Dr. Baker's prediction turned out to be true. From 1969 to 1972, I attended the Custances' Friday night development circle in Brookline, Massachusetts. However, it was not all smooth sailing. After two years with the Custances, I was almost killed in a car accident. Prior to the accident, I had disturbing dream. Gladys Custance, my mediumship instructor, came through in the dream state. As she watched me pick at a splinter in the sole of my foot, she advised "Don't pick at it, let it go." Too late, I was already digging the splinter out with a needle. To my surprise, a cobra came out of the tiny scratch and bit me in the third eye! Even in the dream state, Mrs. Custance was uncannily accurate in her predictions. Two weeks later I was almost killed in a car crash which broke my clavicle into three places, one piece about an inch above my heart.

Of course, I was despondent. My appetite was nil. There seem little to do except to prayer for guidance. One day, I awoke to see Paracelsus written in green letters floating in front of my eyes. When I looked the name up, it was that of a doctor who lived in Europe in the late 1500s. Since Paracelsus believed nature had the power to heal and often suggested that food had curative powers, I broke my fast with a bowl of spaghetti. Little by little my appetite improved and my depression lifted.

Spirit seemed to be guiding me in becoming a medium. In fact, the actual date of my test church service, the final requirement for mediumship had been predicted during an astral travel experience. About three years before, my Hindu master had taken me on an astral travel trip that foretold the event. He began instructing me in astral travel. After the initial few breaths, I felt my spirit leave through my third eye, and float through the ceiling . As I picked up in acceleration, I felt dizzy . Within minutes I was drifting over India and landed in a beautiful pool of turquoise water. When I glanced around, there was my Hindu guide Telepathically, he indicated that I look at a newspaper about twenty feet away. "Draw it near with your third eye," he advised. Concentrating on my third eye, the Sunday edition of the *Boston Globe* was beneath my eyes, with the date April 23 clearly visible. It seems the Hindu had definite plans for me. Three years later, on April 23, 1972, I passed the mediumship service, the final requirement for a certified medium.

Over the years, I have progressed over the years from a mental medium to a trance medium and even added some aspects of physical mediumship-- table tipping and psychic photography. Dreams have continued to play a central role in my life as a professional medium.. That is how the deceased writer, Jack Kerouac entered my life in1990. One night, I had a lucid dream in which I saw him dressed in the stripped robes of an Essene. Kerouac encouraged me in my writing efforts stating emphatically "Fame is on your horizon." Since that 1990 dream, I have written four books on mediumship- *Connecticut Ghosts* and *Séance 101*, *The Making of a Medium*, and *The Art of Mediumship*.

Author: Elaine Kuzmeskus.

Elaine Kuzmeskus has been certified by the National Association of Spiritualist Churches as a Spiritualist medium. During her forty years as a medium, she has conducted many well-publicized séances including the 1997 Official Houdini Séance at the Goodspeed Opera House in Haddam. She has also written four books ***Soul Cycles***, ***Connecticut Ghosts*** , ***Séance 101***, and **The Art of Mediumship**. Recently, she was featured on the PBS special , "Things That Go Bump in the Night."

Chapter One: Famous Dreamers

All our dreams can come true, if we have the courage to pursue them.
Walt Disney

Walt Disney was a dreamer; Art Linkletter a practical man. When Disney drove Linkletter twenty-five miles out of town to look at land for an amusement park, his friend was skeptical. As Walt Disney inspected the large tract of land with only deserted shacks, he insisted "This is the perfect spot for the amusement park-- with plenty of room to put hotels too," Art Linkletter was still not convinced. "Who would drive twenty-five miles for this nutty project?"

Skepticism did not stop Walt Disney from building Disneyland in Anaheim, California, nor did disbelief keep Igor Sikorsky from pursuing his. aviation dreams When Sikorksy was 11, he had a vivid dream of a flying machine kept in the air by numerous propellers. His parents informed their son that such airships did not exist. Disappointed, but not deterred, the child made an invention: "a rotorcraft machine of his own design with a rotor powered by a rubber band." 1 Igor Sikorsky later became famous as the inventor of the helicopter.

Sikorksy had other influential childhood dreams as well. Growing up in Russia far from the ocean, Sikorsky had a recurring dream of flying above an ocean of vivid blue water. It was like no other water he had ever seen on the Russian continent. It was many years before the inventor of the helicopter understood the significance of his dream. According to his son Igor Sikorsky Jr., "Dad was honored to fly Charles Lindbergh to Mexico. When he looked down over the Mexican ocean. there was the incredibly blue water of his dream. "

Thomas Edison like Igor Sikorsky was a prolific inventor and lucid dreamer. In fact, Edison came up with the idea of the electric lamp in a dream. The inventor of the light bulb, liked to nap in his office. "As the story goes, he kept a rocking chair in his office, which he would use for these infamous naps. In one hand he would hold a rock. Beside the chair, underneath the hand with the rock, was a metal pail. The idea behind the pail was that if he fell far enough asleep for the rock to drop out of his hand, the sound of the rock hitting the pail would wake him back up." 2 Edison was often teased about his naps; however,. many new ideas came to him as he slept in his rocking chair on a cot beside his desk.

Another reason Edison was so successful was his work ethic. He was known to toil late into the night in his West Orange laboratory, willing to try many experiments before he achieved results. He believed "Genius is 1 % inspiration and 99 % perspiration." His hard work and "nap" method for obtaining information worked. Edison held 1,093 patents which included one for the electric light bulb, stock ticker, and the recording of music and motion pictures.

Nikola Tesla, a contemporary of Edison's, was also able to tap into dream power. He is best known as the inventor of alternating Current (AC) power systems. Much like today's remote viewers, Nikola Tesla was able to visualize and conduct "dream experiments" while he remained awake in the lab. Apparently he was able to induce a lucid dream state at will. He was so ahead of his time, many of his inventions have yet to be solved.

Dreams have been a source of inspiration for other inventors and scientists.. For instance, Elias Howe received guidance in his dream on developing the needles for his invention, the sewing machine. Physicist, Niels Bohr gained insight into the structure of the atom from a dream: "One night he dreamed of a sun composed of burning gases, with planets orbiting it, attached by fine threads. When he awoke, he realized is was the solution to his puzzle. It explained the structure of the atom and heralded the birth of atomic physics."3

Dr. Bohr was not alone in his use of dreams. Dr. Frederick Banting discovered insulin as a cure for diabetes in a dream. After a long day in his Toronto laboratory, Dr. Banting had a dream in which he saw himself extracting a substance from the pancreas of a dog. When he applied the information obtained in the dream to his research, he discovered insulin!

Many writers have also been inspired by dreams, chief among them Charles Dickens, Graham Greene, Jack Kerouac, and Jules Verne. Dickens received plots, characters, and names in dreams. Coleridge dreamed verbatim his poem, "Kubla Khan". However, he awoke before he received the last lines and was never able to finish the poem. Graham Greene's widow, Vivien, revealed that some of his novels were inspired by dreams. Science fiction writer, Jules Verne, was also inspired by dreams. Author Jack Kerouac wrote a whole book based on dreams, *The Book of Dreams.* His dreams also provided material for his novels, *On the Road* and *The Dharma Bums.* Mark Twain not only received material in dreams but he also met dead relatives and friends in dreams. He even foresaw his own brother's accidental death. In his *Notebook* he described conversation with "the living and dead, rational and irrational."

Stephen King, the horror story writer also found inspiration in his dreams. He told reporter, Naomi Epel: "I've always used dreams the way you'd use mirrors to look at something you couldn't see head-on, the way that you use a mirror to look at your hair in the back." The King of Horror believes dreams an illustrate problems and even provide answers in symbolic language.

Dreams have also inspired architects. In 1883 Don Bosco, an Italian priest, had a dream in which he described a futuristic city that fitted Brasilia's location. The Italian saint said that the city that would be located in the New World, between the 15th and 20th parallels. His vision became the inspiration for the Brazil's modern capital city which was built right on the 15th parallel in Brazil. Brasilia was planned and developed in 1956 with Oscar Niemeyer as the principal architect. And Lucio Costa, the urban planner, an honor he competed for against 5,500 contestants in 1957. On April 22 of 1960, it formally became Brazil's national capital as well as headquarters to many Brazilian corporations. Viewed from above, the main portion of the city resembles an airplane or a butterfly.\

Don Bosco was not the only religious figure inspired by dreams. The Bible is filled with references to dreams and skilled dream interpretation of Joseph and Daniel. The story is that of Joseph with his coat of many colors is one of sibling rivalry, slavery and redemption. When Joseph's brothers became jealous, they stripped him of his finery and sold Joseph into slavery to the Egyptians. Joseph's skill as a dream interpreter became known to the Pharaoh who was plagued by a recurring dream in which he saw seven fat calves followed by seven lean one. Joseph interpreted the dream to mean that there would be seven years of plenty followed by seven years of lean harvests. Joseph won his freedom and saved Egypt from famine.

Daniel was another famous dream interpreter in the Bible. When Nebuchadnezzar, the King of Babylon was troubled by his dreams, he demanded a an interpretation for his dreams or else the mystic would die. Daniel had one day to find a meaning to the dream. That night Daniel had a vision which revealed the meaning. King Nebuchadnezzar received dream about a stone that was cut out from a mountain without hands. The stone rolled down the mountain and destroyed a spiritual image made of gold, silver, brass, iron and clay, and eventually the stone filled the entire earth. The prophet Daniel, said the great stone represented the kingdom of God cut from a mountain without human hands. Eventually the stone would destroy false images and fill the whole earth.5

Dreams seem to be a comfort in troubled times. For example, Joseph the carpenter had after he received a dream when he found out that Mary, his fiancé, was pregnant: "As he contemplated breaking the engagement quietly, an angel of the Lord appeared to him in a dream. "Joseph, son of David," the angel said, "do not be afraid to go ahead with your marriage to Mary. For the child within her has been conceived by the Holy Spirit." 6 Later, the same Joseph , had another dream in which he was warned by an angel: "Joseph son of David, do not be afraid to take Mary home as your wife, because what is conceived in her is from the Holy Spirit" 7

End Notes

1. http://russiapedia.rt.com/prominent-russians/science-and-technology/igor-sikorsky/.
2. http://cocoontobutterfly.blogspot.com/2011/03/meditation-intuition-and-thomas-edison.html.
3 Parker-Hamilton, Craig and Jane*The Psychic Workbook*, Vermillion Press, London, 159.
4. Matthew 2:135.
5. *Holy Bible*, Daniel 2-4.
6. *Holy Bible*, Matthew 1:19-20.
7. *Holy Bible*, Mathew 1:02.

Chapter Two:

Dreams--the Royal Road to the Unconscious Mind

Dreams are the royal road to the unconscious mind-- **Dr. Sigmund Freud**

What do psychologists have to say about dreams? Apparently, they are as fascinated with dreams as everyone else. The father of modern psychology, Dr. Sigmund Freud published The *Interpretation of Dreams* in 1899, and ever since psychologists have been fascinated by dreams. Dr. Freud explained that "Dreams are the royal road to the unconscious mind." Dr..Carl Jung also believed d dreams were the royal road to the unconscious-- and the collective unconscious. Other psychologists: Professor William James, Dr. Louisa Rhine, Dr. Calvin Hall, Dr. Fritz Perls, Dr. Stanley Krippner , Dr. Ann Faraday, Dr. Stephen LeBarge and Dr. Scott Sparrow have shared Dr. Freud's passion for dream analysis.

When Dr. Freud published his book, The Interpretation of Dreams in 1899, he set off a maelstrom of interest in dream interpretation. Freud described four elements of this process that he referred to as 'dream work':

Condensation – Information is reduced into a single thought or image.

Displacement – Emotional meaning is hidden by placing it in other parts of the dream.

Symbolization – Repressed ideas contained in the dream symbolize the hidden meaning of the dream.

According to Freud dreams were a form of unconscious wish fulfillment. The key to interpreting dreams lie in dreams symbols could be interpreted as both manifest, the obvious meaning or disguised meaning which he termed latent. For example, if we dream of a giraffe, the giraffe is the manifest content.. However, the latent content is the symbolic meaning of a giraffe. A giraffe noted for its long neck may be telling the dreamer to view the situation from a "higher perspective" or "overlook" the situation entirely.. Another example, would be a cigar a manifest symbol of tobacco wrapped in a cylinder shape. On a latent level, a cigar, according to Freud's theory, is a phallic symbol.

Freud believed that the mind was like an iceberg—one tenth conscious and nine-tenth unconscious. If the dreamer wishes to tap into the unconscious mind with its repressed desires the psychologist suggested that the dreamer use free association to discover the latent meaning of a symbol. Freud also postulate that displacement of emotional feelings toward one person theoretically could be displaced in dreams to another person . Just as in fairy tales, it is always the step mother who is evil-- never the biological mother. The dreamer does the same thing of distancing by using displacement. For example if the dreamer is angry with his brother, he may dream that his brother is mad at him. Alternately a dreamer may warn his friend, when he or she is the one who needs the advice.

Professor William James, a contemporary of Freud's, took a more mystical approach to dreams by looking at the mind as a "stream of consciousness." James respected the dream state. He explained that dreams have their own region of existence--especially those dreams that "haunt" the dreamer in waking life. While most dreams are quickly forgotten, recurring dreams may be a glimpse to another region: Dr. William James explained "But if a dream haunts us and compels our attention during the day, it is very apt to remain figuring in our consciousness as a sort of sub-universe alongside of the waking world. Most people have probably had dreams which it is hard to imagine not to have been glimpses into an actually existing region of being."1

His lectures published in *Varieties of Religious Experience* gave an in depth look at states of consciousness, including altered states. He did extensive research for the book which included the study of mental healers, psychics, and even nitrous oxide. (laughing gas). "Man exists beyond his individual identity. " James concluded in *Varieties of Religious Experiences:* "Out of my experience, one fixed conclusion dogmatically emerges, there is a continuum of cosmic consciousness against which our individuality but accidental fences and into which our several minds plunge into a sea or reservoir." 2

Carl Jung (1875–1961) believed in a cosmic consciousness which he termed the collective unconscious. He further postulated that his dream symbols balanced whatever elements-- perhaps those of the dreamer's true nature.. Thus In Jung's view, then, dreams are constructed not to disguise forbidden wishes but to reveal They could also serve as a source of healing and sometimes divination. He postulated man possess four types of thought—direct sensation, emotion, reason, and intuition.

Physical sensation	the taste of an orange, touch of a hand
Emotion	elation or depression
Rational thought	ability to reason and comprehend
Psychic	intuitive feelings

Jung's diagram of the personality went beyond Freud's concept of superego, ego and id:

Dr. Carl Jung's Diagram of Personality

Façade

Ego

Shadow

Anima / Animus

Real Self

COLLECTIVE UNCONSCIOUS

Jung felt that the average man was conscious only of the facade or outer personality and the ego. However, beneath the line of consciousness lay a vast unconscious mind which stored repressed desires and fears called the "shadow" or dark side, as well as repressed qualities of the opposite sex termed the anima in males and the animus in females. Going even deeper, one finds the real self at the base of the pyramid, which includes all o the above and more. The task of any individual in this life is bring the real self into consciousness through "memories, dreams, and reflections."

Jung, who did his doctoral thesis entitled "On the Psychology and Pathology of So-Called Occult Phenomena." was fascinated by altered states on consciousness. In his memoir, *Memories, Dreams, and Reflections*, he included dreams he had experienced since the age of four. He also Jung broadened the definition of libido to include psychic energy. Freud, of course, saw the libido as purely sexual. Eventually, Freud and Jung parted ways over the concept of libido.

While Carl Jung shared some commonalities with Freud, he felt that dreams were more than an expression of repressed wishes. He suggested that dreams revealed both the personal and collective unconscious. On one level like Freud Jung dreams served to compensate for underdeveloped parts of waking life.. In other words, dreams bring to consciousness, the unconscious imbalance of suppressed desires of life. Jung explained dreams have deeper meanings. He suggested that archetypes such as the anima(the female principle, the shadow (repressed fears) and the animus (the male principle) are symbolic objects of attitudes that are repressed by the conscious mind. Jung believed that dreams could be highly personal . He felt it was necessary to know the dreamer well in order to fully interpret the dream.

Jung broadened his concept of dreams to include not only unconscious, but mystical experiences from the universal mind which he termed "the collective unconscious". He gave more credence to dreams than Freud and more elegant interpretation to dream symbols. Jung even saw some symbols as archetypes for the soul. Jung defined "archetype" as " the inherited tendency of the human mind to representation of mythological motifs--representations that vary a great deal without losing their basic patterns." For example, the anima was an archetype for femininity, and the animus, an archetype for masculinity. A tree may be an archetype for the tree of life; a ladder, a symbol of ascension or success.

Dreamers can be very selective in their use of archetypes. For instance, a young teacher, Suzanne, living in the United States, had just separated from her boyfriend still living in Europe. Within months of arriving in the United States, she dreamt that she was trapped under Niagara Falls. Since water represents emotion, the dream indicated that she felt overwhelmed with emotion (the falls). However,she could have chosen any body of water to symbolize emotion. Suzanne deliberately chose Niagara Falls because it divides two countries which was the crux of her dilemma.

Much of his life's work was spent exploring Eastern and Western philosophy, alchemy, astrology, and sociology, as well as literature and the arts. His interest in philosophy and the occult Jung wrote that art expression and images found in dreams could be helpful and he often drew, painted, or made objects and constructions at times of emotional distress. He even recommended spirituality as a cure for alcoholism and indirectly played a role in establishing

Alcoholics Anonymous. When Jung treated an American patient (Rowland Hazard III), suffering from chronic alcoholism he the man that his alcoholic condition was near to hopeless, save only the possibility of a spiritual experience. Rowland took Jung's advice and told other alcoholics including Ebby Thache a friend of Bill Wilson, later co-founder of Alcoholics Anonymous (AA). 3

Dreams remain an essential element of study for modern Jungian analysts as well. Dr. Calvin Hall,(1909-1985) who coauthored *A Primer of Jungian Psychology* in 1973, did extensive research on over 50,000 dream reports Hall received his Ph.D. at Berkeley and in1933 he was appointed departmental chair and professor in psychology in 1937 at Western Reserve University. where he remained for the next 20 years. From 1953 on, Hall spent the next three decades of systematic work on dreams. during that period, he developed a cognitive theory of dreams. According to Dr. Hall, dreams express conceptions of the self, family members, friends, and social environment. From his study of 50,000 dream reports, Hall was able to discern a continuity between the dream content and the dreamer's waking life.

One of Dr. Calvin Hall major contributions to dream research was his research in sleep laboratories at the University of California. By using an EEG machine to monitor brain waves, early researchers discovered four stages of sleep. They also discovered that dreams only occur in REM or rapid eye movement sleep. When monitor saw rapid movement in sleep subject and woke the subject up, they inevitable reported a dream. 4 Stages one, two and three of sleep are NREM or non- Rapid Eye Movement sleep:

NREM stage 1: stage between sleep and wakefulness.

NREM stage 2: deep relaxation or theta activity

NREM stage 3: deepest sleep or delta activity

Dream or REM occurs about ninety minutes of the sleep cycle. "This level is also referred to as *paradoxical sleep* because the sleeper, although exhibiting EEG waves similar to a waking state, is harder to arouse than at any other sleep stage. Vital signs indicate arousal and oxygen consumption by the brain is higher than when the sleeper is awake." 5

This research prove scientifically that everyone dreams approximately one-quarter of their sleep cycle. If a sleeper is awakened during the Rapid Eye Movement or REM phase of sleep he or she will report a dream. Dr. Hall divides dreams into five major conflicts in his book, *The Meaning of Dreams.* The first involves feelings toward parents; followed by the conflict of security versus freedom; third ambivalence toward sex roles; the fourth the moral conflict between man's primitive nature and society's expectations; and finally, "the opposing vectors of life and death."

Calvin S. Hall proposed that dreams are part of a cognitive process in which dreams serve as 'conceptions' of elements of our personal lives. Hall looked for themes and patterns by analyzing thousands of dream diaries from participants, eventually creating a quantitative coding system that divided the content of dreams into a number of different categories. According to Hall's theory, interpreting dreams requires more just be understanding the dream. Dream analysis should include analyzing all the elements: the actions of the dreamer, the objects and figures in the dream, the interaction between characters, the setting, and the outcome of the dreamer.

Dr. Fritz Perls (1893-1970) was another modern psychologist interested in dreams. He broke with traditional psychoanalysis, and rejected the notion that that dreams are part of a universal symbolic language. Perls felt that that each dream is unique to the individual dreamer. He also disagreed with the concept of examining the past in detail . Perls favored of a "here and now" approach, along with a more holistic or Gestalt view. In the 1960s, Dr. Perls became well known for his work in Gestalt psychology which takes into account the thoughts, feelings, behavior, body sensations, and dreams focusing on integration.

The psychoanalyst now believed that dreams contain the rejected, disowned parts of the Self. According to Perls, dreams were an "existential message": The dream is an existential message.-- a message of yourself to yourself. Every part, every situation in the dream every aspect of it is a part of the dreamer, but a part that is to some extent disowned and projected on others. If we want to own these parts of our self again, we have to use special techniques by which we can reassimilate these experiences.

Thus, each part of the dream represented part of the dreamer. Frequently, Dr. Perls or Fritz as he preferred to be addressed by his patients, would have a client act out significant parts of the dream. In *Gestalt Therapy Verbatim*, a young struggling artist named Linda learns about herself through dream analysis. In her dream she dives into the water looking for treasure, only to find a heap of garbage. At the bottom of the pile is the "treasure", an old license plate. Which part of the dream did Fritz have Linda role play? The treasure or license plate! Through role playing Linda realized a valuable lesson: "I don't need permission to be creative."

Perls often used an exercise, he called "the empty chair technique" When the client expressed a conflict with another person or in a dream, the client was directed to talk to that another person who is imagined to be sitting in an empty chair beside or across the client. For example, the therapist might say, "Imagine the harsh teacher you saw in your dream is sitting across from you, see her vividly, and, now, talk to her about how it felt to be criticized in your dreams" I the above case of Linda she would put the license plate or any other aspect of a dream, in the empty chair. Ideally, the client should shift back and forth between chairs as to also speak for the person-trait-object in the other chair. Though a dialogue the client can clarify his or her feelings and gain understanding

Since the 1970s, dream interpretation has grown increasingly popular thanks to work by authors such as Ann Faraday. In her book, The Dream Game, Faraday outlined techniques that the lay person could use to interpret their own dreams. Ann Faraday appeared on many radio shows and organized groups for the purpose of recording and interpreting dreams. She believed that by placing little importance on dreams, our society contributed to the poor recall of dreams. Faraday urged her readers to record their dreams immediately upon awakening, lest they forget them. Like Dr. Carl Jung, she was interested in the mystical and mentioned Edgar Cayce's psychic interpretation of dreams in her book.

Stanley Krippner (born1932) an American psychologist, and director of the Maimonides Medical Center Dream Research Laboratory of Brooklyn, New York is also interested in psychic dreams. In 1973, Krippner coauthored *Dream Telepathy* with fellow researcher, Dr Montague Ullman and psychic Alan Vaughan. Vaughan, by the way was the psychic who wrote an urgent letter from Germany a few weeks before assassination of Robert F. Kennedy warning of the upcoming event. In *Dream Telepathy*, Krippner, Vaughan, and Ullman describe dream experiments and the implications of their findings. 6

More recently, Dr. Stephen LeBarge and his colleagues at Stanford University's Sleep Lab have discovered a more fascinating aspect to dreams, the lucid dream. Lucid dreams are vivid dreams in which the dreamer is consciously aware that he is dreaming. These dreams often contain information that goes beyond the consciousness of the dreamer. Lucid dreams have been used to overcome unwanted aspects of the personality such as phobias as well as to probe the future. Researchers such as Dr. Kenneth Ring have a established a link between lucid dreaming and the near-death experience.

Dr. Scott Sparrow in *Lucid dreaming: the Dawning of the Clear Light* explained the significance of lucid dreams and the Divine: "This state of a lucid dream in which the dreamer may enter an illumined state referred in the Tibetan text as the "Dawning of the Clear Light". It is the stage in which the dreamer turns his attention to the Source motivating his dream images" Sparrow goes on to explain this is a state of surrender to the Divine:" The concept of surrender becomes the key to inner illumination and the creative.."

Dream Journal- Part I

It is important to keep a record of your dreams, otherwise they are of little value. When you purchase a journal, look for a thick one to be used exclusively for dreams dictation. Then place it next to your bedside with a pen. Before you go to bed, write the next day's date. You may also wish to write a positive comment or copy an inspiring quotation.

When you wake each morning, write a comment in the dream journal. For instance, "I dreamt that I was back at college," or even "I cannot recall my dream." Just build up the habit of writing each morning. Do not worry about interpreting your dreams at this point. Just record as much detail as possible. Eventually, you will remember more of your dreams in more vivid detail.

However if you go a month without any dreams, you may wish to set your alarm clock for the middle of your sleep cycle on the weekends or any time you do not have to work the next day. Another method is to incubate a dream by waking up fully. Take a ten minutes or so. You could go into the kitchen for a glass or water or juice if you wish. Then go back to bed and try to sleep. Usually, you will go into a dream state. If so, record your dream when you awake. With practice you will awake during a dream, and eventually train yourself to remember your dreams. After you read Chapter Four: Dream Interpretation, you will be ready to decipher your dreams.

Once you have faithfully recorded your dreams. Take time later in the day to analyze their content. First decide if the dream is an important lucid dream or merely a physical dream due to an upset stomach. Some dreams may be decision making dreams such as shopping or viewing a future event.

Next, try to interpret the symbols. What do they mean? For instance if you see a giraffe in your back yard, what does it stand for. Could it be there is a situation at home (back yard) that you need to over look or perhaps see from a higher perspective? Which interpretation fits your life?

Often people dream of being like late for an exam when there is a situation at hand for which they are unprepared. What is going on in your life that feel make require additional attention? When a dreamer is feeling vulnerable, he or she may see themselves as naked or partially clothed. The dream is an indication of vulnerability. Try to figure out who or what is making you feel this way. You can also ask for a follow-up dream to give you strength.

End Notes

1. William James, *The Varieties of Religious Experience*, 1918, Penguin, New York NY, p.294.
2. .William James, *The Varieties of Religious Experience*, 1918, Penguin, New York NY,294.
3. http://en.wikipedia.org/wiki/Carl_Jung.
4. http://www.intuition.org/Vaughan-tribute.htm.
5. http://en.wikipedia.org/wiki/Sleep.
6. http://en.wikipedia.org/wiki/Sleep.

Chapter Three:
The Esoteric Nature of Sleep

When an ordinary man puts the necessary time and enthusiasm into meditation and prayer, he becomes a divine man **Paramahannsa Yogananda**

What actually happens in sleep? Today's psychologists have their own answers concerning the nature of sleep. According to scientific data collected in the sleep laboratories at the University of California under the direction Dr. Calvin Hall the average person sleeps seven to eight hours a night in sleep. During sleep, people go thought four stages: Three of which NREM (non Rapid Eye Movement) stages do not involve dreams. Approximately one quarter of that time is spent in dream or R.E.M. sleep.

What the dreamer is doing the rest of the time may be better understood by a study of esoteric anatomy rather physiology. The inner nature has been a fascinating topic since ancient Egypt. While many see the value in psychological interpretation of dreams, few realize the true spiritual nature of man. This is due in part to the Western emphasis on the physical body without any mention of the astral body. While science continues to learn more and more about the physical body, only a few ancient cultures--notably Egypt, Tibet, India and China-- have made a study of the astral body. . The ancient Egyptians discuss the astral body in The Egyptian Book of the Dead. According to its translator, E.A.

Wallis Budge, the Egyptians believed that "Ka", the astral body . and "Ba", the soul, could leave the physical body at will. They believed this "Ka" or akashic energy was connected to the physical body by cord of " silvery light". Since the cord was etheric, it could lengthen and remain intact even during travel.

There are seven bodies in all-- including the physical, the astral body and the soul. Nature seems to operate on the law of seven. For example there are seven colors in the rainbow, seven notes in a scale, and seven planets in the solar system. According to physicist Hermann von Helmholtz there is also a correspondence between colors and the musical scale.

Musical Notes	**Colors**
G	Ultraviolet
F, F#	Violet
E	Indigo Blue
D#	Cyanogen Blue
D Greenish	Blue
C#	Green
C	Yellow
A#	Orange-red
G#, A	Red
G	Infrared red

Men and woman are also created with Divine intelligence. This spark of Divinity is acknowledged in many culture. It is referred to as "prana" in Vedanta philosophy, "mana" in Hawaiian culture and "Lüng" in Tibetan Buddhism. The Hindus believe that each of the chakra correspond to seven planes of existence: The word "Chakra" literally means wheel and Hindus believe there are seven chakra or wheels of light within the human body These energy centers were first mentioned in the Vedas and the ancient sages advocated opening the chakra through meditation.

Chakra	**Location**	**Goal**	**Element**
7. Sahasrara	top of the head	Cosmic consciousness	Atma
6. Ajna	middle of forehead	clairvoyance	spirit
5. Vishuddha	throat	creativity	ether
4. Anahata	center at heart level	personal love	air
3. Manipura	solar plexus	personal power	fire
2. Svadhisthana	below navel	procreation	water
1. Muladhara	base of spine	survival	earth.

In the East, Hindus believe that when there is balance between the solar and lunar energy bodies, It helps to open the petals of the center for clairvoyance or sixth chakra. The next chakra, the crown is known as "Lotus of a Thousand Petals." Once a student opens this he or she can achieve a trance like state and enter the space between two world. There are some contraindications to opening the chakras as Dr. David Frawley explains in his book *Yoga and the Ayurveda*: "Opening the chakra is not a process for improving one's capacity in the regular domains of human life, thought it may off his as a sidelight, but for going beyond the ordinary condition to a higher evolutionary state." 1 Frawley recommends techniques of pranayana, use of a mantra and meditation to open the chakra. As he explains outer aids such as gem stones and diet can be helpful, but they are subordinate the time honored practice of meditation. According to Dr. Frawley ,"Opening the third eye requires learning to live as pure insight." 2

There are many similarities between the Hindu Chakra System and the Taoist Dan 'tien System, particularly the upper dan tien is similar the Hindu sixth chakra and the third eye, as well as the middle dan tien and the solar plexus area is similar to the third chakra of person power. In ancient China, the energy body was called "chi" Around 475-221 B.C., The Yellow Emperor's Book of Internal Medicine was written. The classic treatise on "chi" is , a dialogue between the emperor and his minister Ch'I-Po regarding questions of health and the healing arts such as acupuncture and the harmony of human spirit with the surrounding world . The "qi " or "chi" is name given to the underlying principle in traditional Chinese medicine and martial arts.

One of the first Western scientist to study the human energy field including aura with some degree of success was , Dr. Walter Kilner. He invented a device to see the aura by using a glass lens covered by a blue die. In 1911, Dr. Kilner wrote a book, *The Human Atmosphere* which explained the aura. experiences. According to his book, Kilner was able to perceive auric formations, which he termed the Etheric Double, the Inner Aura and the Outer Aura.

Sir Oliver Lodge as well as Theosophist, Arthur E. Powell took an interest in Kilner's book. Arthur E. Powell incorporated Kilner's finding in his book "The Etheric Double". While Powell was enthusiastic about Kilner's work, he remade it clear that Kilner had a different view that of theosophists and eastern systems of clairvoyance. Unlike Dr. Kilner who wished to use us knowledge for medical purposed, Arthur E. Powell was interested in pursuing spiritual studies. He believed that the astral body was relatively primitive in an undeveloped man or woman, however in one who was mentally developed the astral body became a means of awakening to the astral and higher planes.

Powell believed that "one of the first things a man learns to do in his astral body is to travel in it, it being possible for the astral body to move, with great rapidity, and to great distances from the sleeping physical body. An understanding of this phenomenon throws much light on a large number of so-called "occult " phenomena, such as " apparitions " of many kinds, knowledge of places never visited physically, ect "3

Theosophist, Charles Webster Leadbeater conducted an extensive study of the chakras outlined in his book, The Chakras. The book, first published in 1927 contains a number of vividly colored, diagrams of energy centers. that serve as psychic sense organs. C.W. Leadbeater acknowledged that each of the seven bodies is attached to one of the seven chakra. He used his clairvoyance to view each chakra and then described each in detail. Leadbeater's own clairvoyance was so remarkable that he was able to peer inside an atom before microscopes were invented that were powerful enough to penetrate the atom's microscopic structure. When microscopes did view the atom, scientists peered into the same structures Leadbeater had described many years before in *Occult Chemistry,* which he coauthored with Annie Besant, the President of the Theosophical Society. "The book consists both of coordinated and illustrated descriptions of presumed etheric counterparts of the atoms of the then known chemical elements, and of other expositions of occult physics" 4

Leadbeater also used his clairvoyant powers to observe the seven chakras and their corresponding body has a particular function. According to Vedic literature, every individual is made up of has seven bodies—physical, etheric, astral, lower mental, higher mental, spiritual, and cosmic consciousness. As a person meditates and lives a spiritual life, the kundalini power at the base of the spine travels up the spine. When the kundalini is raised through the center or charkas of the body, an ordinary person experiences creativity, intuition, and even cosmic consciousness:

	Seven Bodies
Physical body	Three dimensional body
Etheric double	Exact duplicate of the physical body made of finer material.
Astral body	Finer energy body used during the sleep state for astral travel.
Mental body	Finer body which rules consciousness.
Manas	Finer body associated with philosophy and world of creation
Buddhic body	Soul or Individual portion of God.
God or Atma	God or Cosmic consciousness

Leadbeater in his book, Chakras, described their circular nature with spokes of energy radiating from the center. The chakras increase in number of spokes, radiation, and intensity, as they go up the spine from the root chakra with four spokes to the crown chakra known as "the lotus of a thousand petals." The chakras also range in color from infra-red to ultra-violet.

Each chakra has a psychological function as well. For instance, the root chakra with its four petals, keeps the individual grounded. When it is out of balance-- often signaled by lower back pain, the person has security issues. Its color is red and it associated with the fight or fight response to stress.

The second chakra of six petals is located over the spleen, and rules the sex glands. People with a strong second charka exudes warmth. When it is deregulated, sexual indulgence and a desire for glamour and attention can manifest. In the East worldly success is seen as a detriment to spiritual progress.

The third chakra which contains ten petals is located on in the area of the solar plexus. People with a strong third charka has a well-developed intellect, leadership, and confidence. When there is dysfunction, fear and subsequent indecision will reign. Often these indecisive people suffer from stomach problems, especially ulcers

The fourth chakra is located in the center of the chest at the heart level. has twelve petals and is associate with green. It governs the thymus gland, and rules compassion. When this center is depressed, disorders of the heart and immune system, may manifest

The fifth chakra is located in the throat and has sixteen petals rules the thyroid. Its color is turquoise-blue. When opened, it allows for creative thought and clarity of mind..Imbalances in this chakra can cause speech and throat problems. When there is dysfunction, throat and thyroid problems manifest.

The next three chakras have psychic potentials-- the fifth, clairaudience; the sixth, clairvoyance; and the seventh, Cosmic consciousness. This chakra, indigo blue in color, has 96 petals and is associated with the pineal gland. When it is opened faith, spiritual vision and even clairvoyance manifests. However, when it is deregulated, depression, eye problems, and headaches may manifest

The seventh chakra or the crown chakra, has nine hundred and sixty petals and rules the master gland of the body, the pituitary gland. Known in the East as "the lotus of a thousand petals." It is a center for Cosmic Consciousness. However, a soul may experience dysfunction and remain trapped emotionally between the two worlds such as a physical coma or a psychological condition callused schizophrenic which affect one percent of the population. However, when this chakra is opened in a positive manner, the aspirant attains self liberation, freedom from rebirth.

In the sleep state, the physical body with its etheric double remain on the bed while the astral body with its attendant vehicles, tethered to the physical body is free to leave. According to C.W. Leadbeater "Clairvoyant observation bears abundant testimony to the fact that when a man falls into a deep slumber the higher principles in their astral vehicle almost invariably withdraw from the body and hover in its immediate neighborhood. Indeed, it is the process of this withdrawal which we commonly call 'going to sleep'." 5 Often the astral body is directed by desire. "This astral vehicle is even more sensitive to external impressions than the gross and etheric bodies, for it is itself the seat of all desires and emotions — the connecting link through which alone the ego can collect experiences from physical life. It is peculiarly susceptible to the influence of passing thought-currents, and when the mind is not actively controlling it, it is perpetually receiving these stimuli from without, and eagerly responding to them." 6 For example, a mother concerned about an adult child may travel to where he or she is residing to visit. A spiritual aspirant, on the other hand, may go to halls of higher learning on the other side.

Channeler, Edgar Cayce, concurred with much of C.W. Leadbeater's information on the chakra. According to the Sleeping

Prophet, "If a seeker meditates, prayers, and does good for others, he or she raises the energy from the base lower forces of greed, sex and ego to those conditions of love, and spiritual life .Edgar Cayce also believed "the psychic is of the soul". Once the heart center is activated, the spiritual seeker may experience the gifts of the spirit in the form of clairaudience, clairvoyance and even cosmic consciousness g by opening the fifth, sixth and seventh chakras. He often advised people to say The Lord's Prayer as he phase open a different chakra.

Since Cayce's time, physicians such as Dr. Douglas Baker have studied esoteric anatomy. Baker studied the the work of, Alice Bailey who channeled a Tibetan Master. Dr Baker also has his own spirit guide, the Master Robert Browning. From his esoteric studies, Baker has come to the conclusion that "90% of the cause of man's disease lie in planes other than the physical, and it is on those planes that symptoms manifest first before they work through to manifest as gross physical disorders" 7 By using alternative remedies such as Bach Flower Remedies, illness can be treated on the etheric planes.

In the 1960s and 70s Dr. Baker wrote several books on esoteric anatomy and astral travel. According to Dr Baker, we feel in our astral body and think in our mental body. During sleep, we leave our physical-etheric body on the bed, and move about the astral and mental planes in our astral-mental body. "But in deep coma, such as produced by alcohol in any quantity, the astral body cannot leave the physical, cannot in fact come out of alignment with it. It is anchored to the physical body because of the massive metabolic activity going on in the liver and because of the excessive stimulation of the Solar Plexus Chakra resulting from it. "7 Often alcoholics have diminished R.E.M. or dream sleep, as the astral body remains with the physical vehicle.

Later, in1984, Rev. Rosalyn Bruyere wrote *Wheels of Light* which explores the chakra system . She utilized scientific research, Native American culture as well as the tradition of the ancient Egyptians, Greeks, and Hindu philosophy. She founded the

Healing Light Center Church in Sierra Madre, California, and has successfully treated many clients. She utilizes her clairvoyant gifts to view the link between body, mind and soul. For instance, she advised Dr. Jonathan Kramer, a patient who had cancerous tumor "This is pretty big stuff when your body tells you that your job is killing you in a very specific way," says Bruyere. "You're pretty much going to have to deal with all your core assumptions." 8 He followed the advice and survived with a more positive view of life. Rev. Bruyere has also treated many celebrity clients as well: Cher, Barbra Streisand, James Coburn, Frank Zappa, director Martin Scorsese, and, at the very end of his life, Sammy Davis, Jr. and Ellen Burstyn.

Rosalyn Buyere is has an inspiration to many healers including Barbara Ann Brennan, author of *Hands of Light*. Dr. Brennan who is a former NASA physicist draws on both scientific and metaphysical knowledge. In 1987, she established the Barbara Ann Brennan School of Healing. According to Brennan the auric field is the vehicle for all psychosomatic reactions: "The auric field is a quantum leap deeper into our personality than is our physical body. It is at this level of our being that our psychological processes take place. The Human Energy Field is the vehicle for all psychosomatic reactions" 9

In 1984 medical intuitive, Caroline Myss began collaborating with physician Dr. Norman Shealey. Later, in 1996, Caroline Myss, authored *Anatomy of Spirit*. a book which combines the seven Christian sacraments with the seven Hindu chakra. Currently Myss heads Caroline Myss Educational Institute which she founded in 2003. According to its founder, the Institute is "devoted to personal transformation, healing, and the studies of mystical truth." 10

Caroline Myss, Rosalyn. Buryere and Barbara Ann. Brennan have all utilized the knowledge of esoteric anatomy to create health and transformation. They would probably all agree that each of us has the potential to transform through the chakra system. As Paramahansa Yogananda said many years before " When an ordinary man puts the necessary time and enthusiasm in meditation and prayer, he becomes a divine man."

End Notes

1. Michael S. Schneider, A Beginners Guide to Constructing the Universe, Harper, New York: 1994, p. 254.
2. http://www.indiadivine.org/audarya/hinduism-forum/269346-awakening-ajna-chakra.html.
3. http://hpb.narod.ru/AstralBodyByPowell-A.htm#genera.
4. Geoffrey Hodson, An Appreciation of C. W. Leadbeater.
5 http://www.anandgholap.net/Dreams-CWL.htm.
6.http://www.anandgholap.net/Dreams-CWL.htmFor.
7. http://www.amazon.com/Esoteric-Healing-Part -3 ebook
8. http://www.rosalynlbruyere.org.
9.http://www.barbarabrennan.com/welcome/healing_science.html.
10. http://www.myss.com/CMED/about/.

Peace Meditation

When anger or depression enters the thought field, common sense and compassion are quickly negated. People will naturally shut down. On a psychological level, anger is directed outward, while depression is anger turned inward. On an esoteric level, angry emotions are an irritant to the soul , while depressed thoughts siphon its life force. Either way, the ego and its corresponding third chakra suffers. Young people are particularly sensitive and may be influence by the negative emotions of others as well as their own impulsive thoughts. It is possible, however, to shift the negative energy by placing it in a higher chakra with guided imagery.

For instance, when strong emotions of depression block your heart center, try this exercise which was given to the author in her twenties during a period of transition. Dr Douglas Baker suggested that she shift the energy from her solar plexus or third chakra to the heart center which is in the middle of the chest at heart level. The heart chakra is a balance point in the aura and rules the rational mind. Try this calming exercise when life's troubles overwhelm you. It is particular helpful to those who feel that they are in danger of becoming an emotional floor mat for the negativity of those around them.

Sit or lie down in a comfortable position. Be sure to turn the phone off, and pull the shade down so you are in a quiet environment, Have a friend read this script slowly to you. If you prefer, you can read the script into a tape recorder and play it back.

Take a moment to still your body.

Breath in peace.

Exhale all negative emotions.

Repeat three times

Visualize yourself surrounded by white light.

Now, place your dominate hand and place it about six inches from your solar plexus or stomach.

Wait 30 seconds or more until you feel your hand drawing energy.

Bring this energy from your solar plexus to your heart center in the middle of your chest.

Repeat several times, until you feel a shift in energy from excessive emotion to peace of mind.

As you do each sweep slowly, you may wish to add a positive affirmation such as "Divine mind prevails", "I have a God-sound mind in a God-sound body." or "Divine harmony prevails".

Chapter Four :
Dream Interpretation

An unexamined life is not worth living--**Socrates**

Psychics and psychologists alike agree that an unexamined dream has little value. Dreams, particularly vivid dreams are often source of guidance-- if you know how to interpret them. Remember dreams are messages from yourself to yourself. However, sometimes the dreamer is not ready to deal with a situation and may have a dream in which he is here there and everywhere. These dreams are like reading yesterday's newspaper. Interesting, but not that informative. Often the dreamer is trying to make decisions or investigating possibilities, but not ready to make a choice. The same is true of shopping dreams. Here choices are being made as in a grocery shopping scenario.

Another type of dream is one in which the dreamer projects his or her own characteristics onto another person in the dream. This occurs because the dreamer is not ready to face these aspects of within him or her. However, denial usually results in more dysfunction. Take time to study dreams of this nature to be more cognizant of your own short-comings. You will benefit both psychologically and spiritually.

Another variation of dreams is the precognitive dream. Sometimes this dream occurs in a movie theatre setting, Here the dreamer to see himself in a movie theatre looking at a movie. The movie shown on the screen is a preview of coming attractions for the dreamer. In fact, psychic Edgar Cayce stated we often preview important events in a dream first in the dream state. The movie dream is then a dream of the probable future. The clearer the movie, the more probable the future events will be. Cayce, also warn about the importance of fee will. If you do not like what you see, you have the power to change 80 percent of events, don't despair. Ask for a follow-up dream. Often this will come within a week.

Here is an example of dream interpretation Edgar Cayce gave to Morton Blumenthal, who by the way, submitted more dreams to Cayce than anyone else. Blumenthal had this dream: God came to visit him. God was dressed as a modern businessman much to Blumenthal's surprise." Cayce's interpretation pointed out that God was someone with whom we can "do business." God is not only transcendent but also actively involved in human affairs. It was a powerful message and, in a sense, a wonderful revelation from the divine "1

Another widespread dream theme is the exam experience. You rush into class, just as the instructor announces he is giving a surprise quiz. You feel a sense of panic as you have not read the material. This dream is a prototype for anxiety which we have all experienced with surprise tests. The dreamer is sensing that there is a surprise event coming up in his or her life.

Anxiety dreams, it seems are universal while asleep. Many times the dreamer will appear nude or partially clothed. Often no one notices this except the dreamer. The dream represents a feeling of being vulnerable. Notice who is in the dream. For example one young mother who was having problems with her in-laws had a dream in which she was nude from the waist up and having lunch with her brother in law who was unaware of the nudity. Interpretation: the young woman was feeling vulnerable because her brother-in-law who was very critical of her. However, he had not awareness of this. A few months later, the brother-in-law embarrassed her at a family picnic. Rather than fight with him, she just left.

Dreamers frequently report flying dreams-- the dreamer is actually out of his or her body. Often flying dreams are common in childhood, but becomes less so as adults. However, this type of experience can also be symbolic of the desire for freedom or to overcome adversity. In a typical flying dream, the dreamer may visit familiar places or see future events. Some dreamers have even reported flying through the universe. For the most part these dreams are pleasant. Flying can represent out of body experience, as well as contact with the spiritual realm. On a psychological level, flying represents freedom. It can also denote overcoming earthly woes or viewing situation from a larger or higher perspective.

Falling deems are also more typical in childhood. In the falling dreams, though are less pleasant that those of flying. In falling dreams the dreamer watched himself or someone else fall. Often the scene is accompanied by a sense of dread, apprehension, confusion and even panic. A nurse, Janie, who was married with three children had this recurring falling dream: " I saw myself at the edge of a cliff with a baby in my arms. As I stood at the edge of the cliff, to my horror, the baby slipped from the blanket and fell down the cliff. I was overcome with remorse, but there was nothing I could do.

Since the dream was a recurring dream, it was trying to bring through an important message. Later the woman's sixteen year old daughter tried to commit suicide. Apparently when her mother was at work, her father had been sexually abusing her. The dream makes perfect sense. The mother was correctly sensed she was losing a child. By remaining passive, the baby slipped through her arms. Once Janie found out about her husband's sexual abuse, she divorced him and never had the dream again. She had finally gotten the message.

Dreamers may also make direct contact with deceased loved ones in dreams. These meetings usually occur in lucid dreams. Many a spirit just wants the dreamer to know that he or she is alright and there is no need to be concerned. For instance, a forty-one year old woman had in dream in which she was talking to her grandfather. Her impressions were so vivid that she could even feel the bones in his hands as he clasped her. When she woke up, she was just about to ask her husband if her grandfather could move in with them-- until she remembered that he had died twenty years before.

With this knowledge in mind, it is important to interpret the level of the dream as well as the symbols. Sometimes even nightmares can be helpful with the right insight. For example when Belgian comics artist Herger had recurring nightmares in which he was chased by a white skeleton, followed by a whiteout, he consulted a psychiatrist who suggested the artist take a vacation from work. However Herge used the dream material as inspiration for an album set on the snowy mountain tops of Tibet, Tintin in Tibet which was later regarded as one of his finest works. 2 The nightmares, by the way, stopped as he turned his attention to the creation of Tintin.

The famous poet, Samuel Taylor Coleridge, woke one morning having had a fantastic dream (probably opium induced) – he put pen to paper and began to describe his "vision in a dream" in what has become one of English's most famous poems: Kubla Khan. Part way through Poet Samuel Taylor Coleridge was another artist inspired by a dream (54 lines in fact) he was interrupted by **a** "Person from Porlock".

In Xanadu did Kubla Khan
A stately pleasure-dome decree:
Where Alph, the sacred river, ran
Through caverns measureless to man
Down to a sunless sea.

The poem was never finished, though Coleridge returned to it countless time, as he could not remember the rest of his dream. It is important to record a dream as soon as you awake, as within five minutes half of the dream will be forgotten, and ten minutes later about ninety percent.3

Once the dream is recorded, you can interpret it later. Decide first on which level you are dreaming. Then interpret the symbols. People dream on three basic levels--physical, mental or spiritual. An example of a dream influenced by physical reality is one in which the dreamers feels he or she is in typhoon after five slices of pepperoni pizza, a hot fudge sundae and three cups of coffee. The dreamer is incorporating his upset stomach into the dreams If a dreamer is thirsty he or she may dream they are walking on dessert sand. Also on a physical level, men and woman may experience sexual dreams. When these dreams occur males experience erections and females experience increased vaginal blood flow.

The most common level of dreaming, though, is on the mental or emotional level. Men tend to engage in dreams with other men, while woman tend to dream more about other woman. Here is an example of a mental level dream. Heather dreamt that she was riding in her mini van in the back seat, while
her friend, Nancy, was in the second seat. since the two had just had a disagreement, the dream was telling Heather that her friend was putting in last. This later turned out to be true, when the friendship ended.

While mental dreams focus on psychological concerns and physical dreams focus on the needs of the physical body, spiritual dreams often give new information, They may even predict the fate or ink the dreamer with a deceased loved one or spirit guide. In the sleeping state, everyone has the opportunity to cross over to the other side. Mediums, on the other hand, consciously communicate with the other side after years of training. However everyone is psychic in lucid state of sleep.

How do you know if you are having lucid or psychic dream? There are three components. One the dreamer knows he or she is dreaming. Two, the dream is especially clear, often in vivid color. Finally, there is an authority figure present such as monk, a nun, doctor, teacher or police officer. Edgar Cayce advised taking these dreams seriously as they may be taken as warnings, advice, as conditions to be met in order to progress in life.

Psychic dreams often come when the dreamer is facing a crisis. For example, in May of 1988, the author was trying to decide to remain at her job teaching psychology and parapsychology at a local community college. She had this vivid dream in which she was driving over a bridge with two cars behind her. The bridge began to shake and the two cars behind her fell off but the dreamer made it across safely-- though disturbed by the incident. Later, two instructors were let go, but the author still had her job in the Fall.

Once you decide on the level of the dream, you are ready to interpret the symbols. .Dream symbols can be personal ones such knitting needles representing your Aunt Hattie who loved to knit or universal symbols such as a river representing the journey of life.

Take time to notice all the details. If you see a house, it can have many symbols that represent parts of the person who resides within its walls. For example, the front porch is the outer facade shown to the world, while the back door may be secrets which the owner does not wish to share. The basement is the subconscious, while the main floors are the conscious, and the attic the higher mind. The living room represents social life, the kitchen, nutrition, and the bedroom is indicative of sex life and rest.

Even our bodies are symbolic. How often have you heard the expression "The eyes are the "windows of the soul"? The feet are frequently portrayed as symbols of humility, while hearts are drawn to indicate love. We even use the term "blood" to indicate relatives. Colors too have their own unique associations such as seeing "red", feeling "blue," or acting "yellow.". Numbers also have association in common language. We hear that two's company; three's a crowd. Seven is considered to be a lucky number in the West, while nine is viewed as auspicious in the East.

In conclusion dreams can be a direct route to the super-conscious mind or purely physical. However with some practice we can use our dreams for guidance. If you wish to pose a question to the Universal Mind or contact a loved ones or guide on the other side, write your request on a slip of paper. Take a moment to be specific. Put the slip of paper under your pillow, and expect an answer within the next three days. If you do not receive an answer to your query, maybe you have asked the wrong question. Meditate on it and try rewording the original question or asking another one. With practice, dreams can provide guidance to life's most perplexing issues.

Dream Symbols

Animals

bee	industry or "stings" of life
bear	highly protective especially of family members
beaver	hard worker
bugs	minor irritations
bull	stubborn, highly sexed
butterfly	transformation , reincarnation, joy
cat	independent, or "catty" -critical, psychic (Egyptian)
cow	bossy, overweight
deer	gentle, kind
dog	loyal, friendly
donkey	humble, determined
horse	a messenger
giraffe	higher perspective, gentle
lamb	spring, Christ
lion	pride
lady bug	good luck
lizard	gossip,
monkey	immature, funny
pig	selfish
rabbit	fast, sex
sheep	shy, sleep
shark	aggressive, dishonest
skunk	resentment, a spoiler
snake	change, evil, sexual, gossip, wisdom, kundalini

spider	entrapment
tiger	power, severe attitude
turtle	slow, long life (American Indians)
wolf	sexual predator
worm	lower energy, destructive attitude

Birds

bluebird	happiness
chickencoward	
dove	peace
duck	sense of humor, "ducking" the issue
eagle	vision, high standard, legal field
goose	folly
hen	motherly, protective
hummingbird	psychic as a messenger between the two world, (American Indian), joy
hawk	indicate a condition that needs to be watched carefully
owl	wisdom
parakeet	love bird
robin	spring, new beginning
rooster aggressive,	domineering
peacock	pride, vanity, clairvoyance
vulture death	

Body

back	will
bladder	anger or "pissed off"
blood	close relative
breasts	nurturance
chest	feeling, heart center

ears	listening, big ears stubborn
eyes	vision," windows of the soul"
feet	humility, balance
hair	thinking: golden hair, spiritual; red hair, temper; white hair, wisdom; unkempt hair, mental unbalanced; bald, need for new ideas.
hands	work ; shaking hands, friendship
knees	humility; stiff knee, the need to be more flexible
legs	moving forward
lips	speech
mouth	communication: thin lips, tight speech, full lips, warm
neck	connection, creative will
stomach	assimilation, digestion, or something you can't stomach, solar plexus, personal will
teeth	speech: loose teeth, careless speech, crooked teeth, dishonest speech, sharp teeth, cruel speech, brace , need to watch your word, falling teeth, too talkative

Buildings

airport	travel, high ideas
apartment	temporary dwelling, transition
bank	security, treasure
church	spiritual state
court	karma, justice
store,	"shopping around", ,decisions
door	opportunity: front door, positive, back door, behind the scenes or secret;
fence	obstacle, boundary may be needed
grocery store	diet, nutrition
hallway	transitions, relationship
hospital	health, healing

house	basement, foundation; attic, higher mind; porch, facade, back of house, hidden side of home; burning house, poor health or anger;
motel	vacation, temporary condition, transition
rooms	living room , social life; bedroom, sex or rest; kitchen, nutrition; unfinished rooms, areas of life that are incomplete; many rooms, expanding consciousness or spiritual life
bathroom,	cleansing., dining room family gathering
school	learning
shack	poverty, railroad station shack, a trip
tower	higher mind
tunnel	subconscious
wall	obstacle or separation

Clothing

clothes	ego, work consciousness: clean clothes, honest work; spoiled clothing unethical; , tight garments, restricted thought, mean spirited
coat	protection or need for protection
hat	thinking
jewelry	treasures, luxury, generous
rings	union, wedding, commitment
shoes	new condition, hole in shoe, a problem in need of
repair	

Colors

red	vital physical energy, sex, anger, in debt, stop
pink	joy, pale pink, lack of courage, rose, very positive
orange	pride, courage, sacred color in the East
yellow	sunshine, cheerfulness, pale yellow cowardice
green	harmony, health, patience
blue	sky, spiritual color, blue or sad mood

purple	royalty, unique, older person
white	purity, medical field, spiritual
black	void, negative, death, mystery, black and white, right or wrong . karma
grey	unsure, worry , illness
brown	earthy, practical, materialistic

Common Symbols

baby	new start
badge	authority
book	knowledge
boulder	obstacle
bridge	transition, relationship
cake	celebration, birthday
car	transportation, dreamer
cave	mediation
circle	unity
clock	time
coins	money
death	an ending
flag	military service
harp	music, harmony, Ireland
ladder	success, desire to advance
moon	psychic, mystical, feminine
music	harmony rainbow psychic
sand	shifts
sun	recognition, attainment, masculine
pen	writing
telephone	communication
woods	confusion

Flowers

In general flowers symbolize joy, beauty and happy occasions.

daffodil	spring, golden opportunity
daisy	youth, decision making
fleur de lis	spirit of France
lily	Easter, rebirth
lotus	blossoming, enlightenment, crown chakra,
	morning glory resurrection
rose	love, Mother Mary
pansy	mother, remembrance, humility
sunflower	joy, symbol of Spiritualism
shamrock	luck, symbol of Ireland, Holy Trinity

Gems and metals

amethyst	royalty psychic energy, spiritual healing
diamond	leadership "king of gems" good luck
emerald	physical healing, peace, prosperity
gold	king of metals, relates to God, attainment, the Sun
jade	Orient, improves life force
lapis,	Egypt, enhances spiritual and psychic force
pearl	feminine , purity, fertility
sapphire	spiritual, high minded, spiritual, confidence
silver	queen of metals, relates to Goddess, Moon and
fertility	
ruby	high earthly attainment, riches, energy
rose quartz	love, heart center, improves circulation
turquoise,	American Indian, tranquility

Numbers

one	God, , unique, pioneer
two	a couple, balance
three	manifestation, Holy Trinity
four	four-square, secure, obstacles

five	pentacle, magic, creativity, change
six	service , humility
seven	spiritual number, completion of t individual cycle, good luck
eight	two fours, obstacles, security that is earned
nine	travel, adventure, guru in the East , lucky
ten	interpret as one
eleven	double number stays the same, lucky for goals
twelve	spiritual number, represents completion for a group
thirteen	twelve plus one, an occult number, at times, unlucky number

Trees

birch	new beginning
bonsai	harmony and balance
cedar	healing
cypress	hope
cherry tree	rebirth
Christmas tree	celebration, hope
elm tree	strength, stability
evergreen	Christmas, remembrance
fruit	abundance, happiness
maple tree	practical
oak	strength
palm tree	relaxation, life after death
pine	protection, longing for someone
weeping willow	sorrow

Situations

barefoot	unprotected
bathing	cleansing
birth	new condition
death	condition that is ending

fishing	spiritual life
flying	wishful thinking, freedom, astral travel
fork in the road	decision making
marriage ceremony	wedding or spiritual union
naked	feeling vulnerable ear espoused
running	escape
skating on thin ice	danger
swimming	spiritual activity
weeping	warning of trouble

Dream Journal Part II

Once you have faithfully recorded your dreams. Take time later in the day to analyze their content. First decide if the dream is an important lucid dream or merely a physical dream due to an upset stomach. Some dreams may decision making dreams such as shopping or viewing a future event.

Next, try to interpret the symbols. What do they mean? For instance if you see a giraffe in your back yard, what does it stand for. Could it be there is a situation at home (back yard) that you need to over look or perhaps see from a higher perspective? Which interpretation fits your life?

Often people dream of being like for an exam when there is a situation at hand for which they are unprepared. What is going on in your life that feel make require additional attention? When a dreamer is feeling vulnerable, he or she may see themselves as naked or partially clothed. The dream is an indication of vulnerability. Try to figure out who or what is making you feel this way. You can also ask for a follow-up dream to give you strength.

End Notes

1. http://near-death.com/experiences/cayce14.html.
2. http://www.here-be-dreams.com/famous.html.
3. http://www.here-be-dreams.com/famous.html.

Chapter Five:
The Psychic Side of Dreams

All day long I have exciting ideas and thoughts. But I take up in my work only those to which my dreams direct me. **Dr. Carl Jung**

Dr. Jung examined the dreams of his patients as meticulously as he did his own dreams. He knew that dreams can come true-- especially if you examine the psychic side of dreams. This includes ESP, telepathic dreams, warning dreams, as well as direct communication from the other side of life. Psychic dreams can also take the form of precognition, clairvoyance, telepathy and even after-life communication. Precognitive dreams tell the dreamer the probable future in a direct fashion or through symbols. Many psychics believe that these dreams give the dreamer the chance to change their future-- if the dreamers takes them as a warning ahead of time.

Such was not the case for President Abraham Lincoln. 1865, two weeks before his assassination, Lincoln had a precognitive dream about a funeral in the East Room of the White House. The President told his wife of his sickening surprise. "Before me was a catafalque on which rested a corpse wrapped in funeral vestments. Around it were stationed soldiers who were acting as guards, and there was a throng of people, some gazing mournfully upon the corpse.' When the Abraham Lincoln asked "Who is dead in the

White House," one of the soldiers answered "The President. He was killed by an assassin."1 Sadly, Lincoln did take his psychic dream seriously for on Good Friday, April 14, 1865, the President gave his bodyguard the night off.

American author, Mark Twain, also had a premonition about his brother Henry's death in a dream. One night he saw his brother's body in a metal coffin supported by two chairs with a white vase with crimson flowers in it. Weeks later Henry was killed in an explosion on his riverboat. When Mark Twain went to identify the body, there it was in a metal coffin purchased by a local woman who was moved by the sight of Henry's young face. There was no vase with red flowers, however as Mark Twain stood over the coffin, a woman rushed in with a bouquet with a single red rose in the middle. 2

Dreams also played an important role in the life of a contemporary of Twain's Daniel Douglas Home. Home (1833 –1886) was a Scottish physical medium who was known for his ability to levitate, to produce rappings and knocks in houses at will, as well as communicate with the death. He first found out that he was a medium in a dream. Home's best friend who lived three hundred miles away came appeared in the dream with a message that he had died. Home was not surprised when he was told of his friend's death the next day. 3

Larry Dweller, author of *Beginner's Guide to Mediumship* also became interested in mediumship through a dream. When he was fourteen, Dweller dreamt of -a deceased relative.

"One dapper gentleman dressed in a hound's-tooth suit and white spats appeared regularly in my dreams, usually delivering lectures on the importance of homework and imparting advice on how to get along with family members." Later he spied the dapper gentleman in a family album- it was his grandfather who died in 1932! 4

Another author, Ann Rice, dreamed that her young daughter had died of a blood disease. Soon after her dreams, Rice's daughter was diagnosed with leukemia. "In the aftermath of her daughter's death, Rice wrote *Vampire* in a feverish frenzy in just three weeks, as though it were a kind of purging." 5

Naturally, Ann Rice would have given anything to save her daughter. However, sometimes it is possible, other times not. For instance, many people have premonitions of major events such as Titanic which sunk in 1912 and the demise of twin towers in New York City, yet few report them-- and if they do, their psychic dreams are not take seriously. Two years before 9/11, Phyllis Sergeant , whose husband was a fire chief in a small town in Connecticut had a dream in which she saw several firemen from her husband's firehouse rushing into New York City. "They had full gear with a look of fear in their eyes." Phyllis just "knew" that there would be an explosion in New York, so wrote a detailed letter of her premonition to the FBI, but never received a response from the agency.

Another form of psychic dream is that of dream telepathy in which one communicates telepathically with another in a dream. Sigmund Freud was one of the first people to record such dreams. He presented a paper on the subject, "Dreams and Telepathy" in 1922. Since Dr. Freud had never experienced a telepathic dream, he labeled those who did as experiencing as "purely subjective anticipations" However, Dr. Carl Jung considered telepathic dreams within the concepts of dream transference.

Later, psychologist, Dr. Stanley Krippner experimented with dreams at the Maimonides Medical Center in Brooklyn New York in 1964. Dr. Krippner set up a triad with a sender, a receiver. and a monitor. Once the receiver was in REM sleep, the monitor woke the sender who would then concentrate on images to the sleeping receiver. After 15 minutes, the monitor woke the receiver and recorded his or her dreams. "According to Stephen Phillip Policoff in *The Dreamer's Companion*, of the twelve studies complete from 1966-1972, nine showed considerable accuracy between images sent and received."6

In clairvoyant dreams the dreamer is not receiving information from another person as in a telepathic dream. Instead, the dreamer sees an event as it is happening. The details are factual with experience of images and sounds or voices Unlike precognitive dreams, where there some chance of changing fate, there is no way to prevent what is happening in a clairvoyant dream. An example of a clairvoyant dream would be seeing an earth quake in Peru as it is occurring while the dreamer is asleep in the United States.

Sometimes we visit locations in dreams before we do in real life. For instance, a middle-aged devotee of Sai Baba, Eileen had a dream in which she saw the door to a hotel room with the numbers two one two on it. When she arrived at her hotel room for a Sai Baba conference, she was given a key to a second-floor room. Sure enough, the room had gold letter 212 across the door. Many times, people feel a sense of déjà vu on visiting a new place, most probably because they have already visited in their dreams as Eileen did.

The most intriguing dreams involve contact with people who are dead. Often these people appear as they were at the time of death, however, many times they will appear younger and healthier. For instance, Ed Kellogg had a lucid in which he was looking for his elderly friend, Bruno, a bald, paunchy gentleman who dressed casually. In the dream Bruno looked a fit forty year old dressed in a grey suit-- and his frizzy white hair is cut short. Later Kellogg was able to verify the details of the accuracy of Bruno's younger appearance from a photo taken when Bruno was in his forties. As for the suit, according to his son, his father was buried in a grey suit! 7

Many a medium has described the deceased as a younger and more vital in appearance. Often this indicates that departed person is at peace and able to turn back the hands of time. Some spirits such as those of ancient sages prefer to maintain their distinguished, older appearance. However most like to return to their 30s and 40s. For example, when the author saw Rev. Carl Hewitt in spirit, the seventy--six old medium appeared in a dapper blue sports coat and a Florida tan. He had the health and happiness of a man in his forties.

Frequently, the departed only wants to let the family that they should get on with their lives. Grief, apparently, holds back not only those who mourn, but the deceased as well. In the book, *Paula,* Isabel Allende described her recurring dreams of her daughter, Paula, who died at 28. After Paula died, her spirit frequently appeared in Allede's dreams dressed in a white night gown and slippers. The reason? Paula wanted her mother to stop grieving as her grieving was holding Paula back.

Isabel Allende is not alone in her ability to communicate with the spirit of her deceased daughter. In *Hello From Heaven*, Bill and Judy Guggenheim give 350 first-hand accounts of people who have received messages from their departed loved ones. In most cases the messages were given to reassure loved one that their deceased relative was alright. When the after-death communication occurred in dreams they were vivid and intense, more real than an ordinary dreams. Typically the dream included two-way communication as well.

Dr. Ian Stephenson gave an example of this in his book *Children Who Remember*. One girl who had been killed in an accident, Ranjani, was anxious to return to her mother. The child came through in her mother's dream to tell her that she wished to be reborn. "Rajani's mother , however, did not wish to have another child and induced an abortion. The deceased child appeared again in a dream, and rebuked her mother for not letting her reincarnate. Eventually, the mother consented and gave birth to Rajani who later remembered the life of her older sister." 8

Unlike dreams of death and dying, these dreams are a source of comfort-- often seeming more like a visit than a dream. According to Rosemary Ellen Guiley, author of *Dreamspeak*, divides after-death communication into three categories--"the farewell", "the reassurance", and "the gift." Guiley explains "Themes within these types of encounter dreams are the eternal bonds of love; forgiveness, blessings; assurances; gifts; and information about the Other Side."9 It makes sense that loved one wish to say a final good-bye.

After-death Communication

Many mourners report contact with their loved ones in dreams. Often the spirit is trying to reassure their grief-stricken that death is not the end of the relationship. Widows often report that they have had dreams of their departed husband urging them to go on with their lives. Also, it is not unusual for parents to be comforted by deceased child in a dream. Just seeing the face of a loved one can be healing.

Often people who have lost a family member or a friend receive comfort from a session with a medium. While it is gratifying to make contact with your loved ones through a psychic medium, you don't really need an intermediary. It is entirely possible to communicate with those on this side through dreams.

Before you go to sleep, send the thought out to your loved one that you wish to be in contact. Have faith, that when spirit is ready, he or she will come into your dreams. However, you do need to take a moment each morning to write your dreams down. Otherwise, you are likely to miss vital details of the spiritual visitation.

It is also a good idea to date these dreams and underline the names of departed loved ones As you become more conscious of your dreams, you will see how thin the veil between the two worlds really is.

End Notes

1. http://worldofspirit.blogspot.com/2009/01/psychic-abilities-abraham-lincoln-and.html.
2. http://www.world-of-lucid-dreaming.com/precognitive-dreams.html.
3 Jon Klimo, Channeling, Jeremy Tarcher, Los Angeles, CA 1987, page 191.
4. Beginner's Guide to Mediumship, Larry Dweller, Weiser Books, York Me, 1997, page 4.
5. *The Everything Dream Book,* by Trish and Rob Macgregor , Adams Media, Avon MA 1997, page 98.
6. *Idiot's Guide to Interpreting Your Dreams* Penguin Group, New York NY 2003, page 253.
7. *Lucid Dreaming,* Robert Waggoner, Moment Point Press, Needham MA,2009, p 238-239.
8. *Dreamspeak*, Rosemary Ellen Guiley, Berkeley Books, New York NY 2003, page 253.
9. Dr. Ian T. Stevenson, *Children Who Remember*, McFarland and Company, Jefferson NC, 2001 page 248.

Chapter Six
Dream Healing

The dream world is the real world. **Seneca Indian healer.**

Westerners may give very little thought to the dream body. The Aborigines, however, pay a great deal of attention to dreamtime where the spirits dwell between life times: "Both before and after life, it is believed that this spirit-child exists in the Dreaming and is only initiated into life by being born through a mother. The spirit of the child is culturally understood to enter the developing fetus during the fifth month of pregnancy."1 Thus, traditional Aborigines embrace dreamtime and utilize knowledge gleaned in dreams for personal guidance and community rules.

According to dream expert, Robert Moss, "The Iroquois Indians also believe in "big dreams" They believe that "the dream soul can go far and wide, into the future or the past to places at a great distance from the dreamer's body, into the hidden dimensions of reality, where it encounter the spirit guides or ancestors."2 The Iroquois looked carefully for supernatural signs, and took time to interpreting these dreams. For the Iroquois, dreams were indicators of the soul's direction in life. To ignore dream guidance was to court misfortune.

Unfortunately few Western physicians believe in dream guidance however some are looking into the energy or light body which is detailed in the Chinese system of acupuncture. Recently, the National Institute of Health gave their approval for the use of acupuncture for certain ailments: "Researchers don't know how these ideas translate to our Western understanding of medicine, explains Dr. Richard L. Nahin of NIH's National Center for Complementary and Alternative Medicine. "but the fact is that many well-designed studies have found that acupuncture can help with certain conditions, such as back pain, knee pain, headaches and osteoarthritis." 3

While modern doctors are now beginning to explore the energy field, ancient physicians knew about the energy field. They acknowledged there were seven bodies. The ancients also paid close attention to dreams in their healing practices. For example, the ancient Egyptians even believed that they could contact the gods who served as oracles in dreams. Often the ancient Egyptians would travel to famous temples such as the temple at Memphis. Here they would sleep in the hope of reviewing a dream revelation. Ancient Roman took dreams so seriously that "Emperor Augusts Caesar ruled that anyone who had a dream about the state was, by law, to proclaim it in the marketplace. "4

Both the Romans and Greek of the ancient world took dreams seriously as messages from the gods. The Greeks also believed in dream incubation and insisted on purification before interring the temples. "Two days before entering the shrine (Shrine of Apollo at Delphi) they abstained from sex, ate no meat, fish or fowl, and drank only water. In addition an animal sacrifice was made to the god whom they wished to invoke through a dream." 4 Then the dream would sleep in the skin of the sacrificed animal in the hopes of contacting to contact the God of Healing Ascepelius."

Approximately 320 temples dedicated to Asclepius were scattered throughout the known Hellenic world. from around 1300 BCE to 500CE. If a Greek physician was unable to cure an illness his patient would be sent to one of the many healing temples dedicated to Asclepius, the son of mortal woman and the god Apollo. He was revered for as a Divine physician. "So good were his powers to heal that the gods feared he was denying the 'underworld' of souls and was struck down by lightning. Such were the cries from the human world that Asclepius was deified by Zeus."5

For over 2,00 years these healing sanctuaries offered were often away from the populace in lovely country setting. In these calm environments, the patient enjoyed nutritious food, music theater and help from the temple attendant called therrapeutes. The god could heal directly with dream surgery or by giving advice. Greek dream healing was apparently quite successful In the 2nd Century C. E.Pausanius a noted travel writer describe the tablets in the entryway of Epidavr: On these tablets are engraved the names of men and women who were healed by Asclepius, together with the disease from which each suffered, and how he was cured "6 The most Amazing healings occurred: a "voiceless boy spoke, paralyzed limbs and fingers were freed from affliction, and others left without pain. One man even had surgery: "Gorgias of Heracleia was with pus. In a battle he had been wounded by an arrow into lung and for a year and a half had suppurated so badly he filled sixty seven basins with pus. While sleeping in the temple he saw a vision. It seemed to him the god extracted the arrow point from his lung. When day came he walked out well, holding the point of the arrow."7

Hippocrates, the father of modern medicine, was the son and grandson of Askplepian priests. He believed both mind and body were important in healing and utilized dreams for assistance in diagnosis and treatment Years before. Sigmund Freud, Hippocrates who founded his medical practice in the 4th century B.C.E. was one of the first physicians who tried to provide a scientific account of dreams. Hippocrates believed that dreams were significations of psychic problems. "A dream about eating for example, meant that the dreamer was suffering from depression and was trying to make up for some deficiency. A psychoanalyst thousands of years later would interpret a dream of this nature the same way, with the exception of calling the dream an example of "compensation." 8

Psychotherapist, Dr. Carl Jung placed more stock in dreams than did Freud. He used dream analysis to resolve emotional or religious problems of this patients. Jung wrote that recurring dreams show up repeatedly to demand attention, suggesting that the dreamer is neglecting an issue related to the dream. Jung believed that memories formed throughout the day also play a role in dreaming. Jung called this a day residue."9 He would term a healing dream "a big dream" as opposed to everyday dream which are of little consequence. Jung belied these big dreams to be important breakthrough to the unconscious mind. By taking time to study important dreams, the dreams can connect with archetype and symbols to heal mind and ultimately body.

Dream authorities also feel that dreams can also help the dreamer avoid potential health issues: "Research shows that asthma and migraine sufferers have certain types of dreams before an attack. Your bodies are able to communicate to your mind through dreams. The dreams can "tell" you that something is not quite right with your bodies even before any physical symptoms show up" 10 Dreams of this type can be invaluable in getting the dreamer to a doctor or dentist in the early stages of illness for treatment.

Dreams can serve as an early warning system for psychological problems as well. Maggie, One mother of four grown children was visiting her son on Thanksgiving. She was miffed when she went downstairs in the basement of his home to smell marijuana. Wisely, she kept her suspicions to herself. The next night, she heard a man's voice speak to her in her dreams "Drop it " he advised . While not happy with the situation, she realized this was sound advice.

Psychotherapist and Viet Nam vet Dr. Ed Tick believes that "Any condition of the mind, body or spirit can be treated by Asklpian healing."11 In his book *The Practice of Dream Healing*, he described the psychotherapy as well as shamanic practices he has used with many veterans For example, Dr. Tick used a fire ceremony to assist vets from the Catskill veterans center able make peace with their fallen comrades. According to Tick, "among Native American people and some other warrior traditions lit watch fires to guide their wandering warriors and hunters home. We built our watch fires for lost spirits of the veterans dead companions, and said prayers, told stories and cried out for them to return home." 12

Another patient of Dr. Tick's a nurse who was suffering from PTSD. She was so haunted by the faces the Viennese children she could not save that she fled to Canada. During her dream healing, the children who haunted her sleep came back to tell her "You are our mother . You tried to give us life." Her anxiety was reduce 80 percent and she was able to get of f her PTSD 13

Ed Tick is not alone in his belief in the healing power of dreams Shaman Sandra Ingerman received a profound healing in her dreams , At the time, she was suffering from chronic pain and she prayed for a healing in a dream. After praying over a month, she received her request: " At last she dreamed that a Native American man emerged from behind the sofa in her living room, holding a translucent blue rattle. He pointed the rattle at the part of her body where she was in pain. He shook the rattle over that place until the pain in her dream body was gone "15 Miraculously she awoke to a pain-free body.

Another Shaman, Dr. Alberto Villodo, who studied with the shamans of the Andes and Amazon concurs with Dr. Ed Tick and Sandra Ingerman's view of dream healing: "The fact is, you can live the life of a victim, burdened by the traumas of your past, or you can live the life of a hero, but you can't do both. If you want to feel empowered, you need to make a conscious decision to dream a sacred dream and practice courage."16

Shamanic dreaming is a powerful technique" It can be used to see into the future, as well as the world of spirits. When used correctly shamanic dreaming can heal old psychological wounds and create a more positive future. You can enter the dream state through Shamanic drumming , the flute music of the South American Indians. Shamanic Journey Solo and Double Drumming by Michael Harner or Canyon Trilogy: Native American Flute Music by R. Carlos Nakai.

Shamanic Dreaming

Start by setting aside a regular time for this exercise. Prepare the room by smudging with sage or incense. Begin with a prayer of intention such as Divine light surrounds me on my journey to_________________. You fill in the blank with your intention. You may wish seek guidance, desire to contact a spiritual guide , ask for healing.

You may wish to lie or sit on a meditation cushion or mat to buffer against unwanted earthly influences. Once you are comfortable, play the gentle music, start your mediation cd for 10 to 15 minutes. As you allow your body to relax into the music , the sound becomes your conduit to the dream zone. Eventually you will enter a light dream-like trance state as the body relaxes. At this point, you will enter a conscious state of dreaming, accompanied by an inner feeling of clarity. With practice the Shamanic dreamer enters a state in which visions come and deep healing occurs. Shamanic dreamers also report visual or auditory sensations—perhaps seeing vivid colors or hear spiritual . They may also come in contact with loved ones or even spirit guides.

Shamanic dreams can be very helpful-- providing the dreamer can remember the journey, so take time to write down all the details of your shamanic dream as soon as you finish the session.

End Notes

1 http://en.wikipedia.org/wiki.
2. Robert Moss, *Conscious Dreaming*, Three Rivers Press, New York, NY page 14.
3. .http://newsinhealth.nih.gov/issue/feb2011/feature1.
4. http://library.thinkquest.org/26857/historyofdreams.htm.
5. http://library.thinkquest.org/26857/historyofdreams.htm.
6. http://www.dreamhealinggreece.com/ancient%20and%20 modern.html.
7. 4http://www.dreamhealinggreece.com/ancient%20and%20 modern.html.
8. http://www.examiner.com/article/significance-of-dreams-according-to-ancient-civilizations.
9. http://www.dreamviews.com/wiki/Dream-Content.
10. http://www.dreammoods.com/dreaminformation/dreamtypes. http.
11. http://www.shamansociety.org/tick.pdf .
12. http://www.shamansociety.org/tick.pdf.
13. http://www.shamansociety.org/tick.pdf .
14. healing quest. http://www.shamansociety.org/tick.pdf .
15. http://blog.beliefnet.com/dreamgates/2011/07/ shaman-as-dreamer-talking-with-sandra-ingerman. html#ixzz2DANOdWDz.
16. http://www.openexchange.org/archives/JFM08/villoldo.html.

Chapter Seven:
Divine Intervention

Go up to the mountains and breath the air the angels breathe.
Naturalist John Muir

According to the Bible and the texts of ancient Egypt, Rome, Persia, and India, divine intervention is a reality that frequently comes in the form of angels. For the mystic, they exist in the inner realms; the naturalist in nature. John Muir, who knew well the majesty of nature, advised "Go up to the mountains and breath the air the angels breathe"

The word *angel* is of Greek origin meaning messenger . Ever since Biblical times, people have believed in their divine intervention. Both the Old Testament and the New Testament abound in stories of angels. For instance, angels who appeared to Abraham as he sat in the shade of his tent.1 They appeared like ordinary travelers with dusty feet. Jacob also received a visit from an angel in human form. Jacob wrestled with the angel all through the night. Eventually the angel blessed Jacob and changed his name to Israel.

In the New Testament the angel Gabriel tells Mary she is with child: "And in the sixth month the angel Gabriel was sent from God unto a city of Galilee, named Nazareth, To a virgin espoused to a man whose name was Joseph, of the house of David; and the virgin's name was Mary. And the angel came in unto her, and said,

Hail, thou that art highly favored, the Lord is with thee: blessed art thou among women. " 2, Naturally Mary was troubled by Gabriel's message, the angel told "fear not" as she had found favor with God.

Later an angel of the Lord spoke to Joseph in his sleep to warn him to flee into Egypt . Joseph was told only to return to Israel after the death of King Herod who sought to kill baby Jesus. Jesus also spoke of angels. One particular on -- probably Gabriel appeared to him twice by the River Tigris. Even after his death two angels in shining white robes appeared to Mary Magdalene, as she stood weeping at the tomb, stooped down and looking in, "saw two against in white, sitting, one at the head, and one at the feet, where the body of Jesus had been laid." 3

Visions of angels often come in times of trouble. For instance, a thirteen year old girl heard voices in the summer of 1425. The maid, Joan of Arc discerned the blaze of light that accompanied the voice to St. Michael the patron saint of the royal house of France. At first the messages were more personal, followed by urgent pleas for the nation. According to Joan of Arc, "He told me Saint Catherine and Saint Margaret would come to me, and I must follow their counsel; that they were appointed to guide and counsel me in what I had to do, and that I must believe what they would tell me, for it was at our Lord's command." 4. When Saint Michael commanded Joan to go to the aid of France which she did. In May 1428, she received the order to . to go to the King of France to help him win his kingdom back. After overcoming opposition from both clergy and court,, the seventeen year old girl was allowed a small army to seize Orleans on May 8, 1429. While her military successes were spectacular, she remained a naive teenager. Sadly, the nineteen year old was trapped into giving false testimony and was condemned to death as a heretic, sorceress, and adulteress, and burned at the stake on May 30, 1431. 5

During the first world war, there were reports Joan of Arc as well as angels coming to the aid of France: When the British Expeditionary Force arrived in France on August 22-23,1914, they were outnumbered by German soldiers at the Battle of Mons, yet they forced the German Army into retreat. Those with military knowledge wondered about such an outcome. On 24 April 1915,a British Spiritualist magazine published an account of supernatural forces present. "Descriptions of this force varied from it being medieval longbow archers alongside St. George to a strange luminous cloud, though eventually the most popular version came to be angelic warriors" 6

Angels also play a strong role in psychic Edgar Cayce's life. When he was ten years old, he received his first visit from an angel. The young boy was paralyzed with fear and astonishment when a "beautiful woman" appeared.. She asked the child what he would like? He answered " I would like to help others especially children." Edgar Cayce went on the become a medical trance medium and gave 14,000 readings-- 116 are "work " reading regarding how Cayce should carry out the day to day and spiritual nature of his work. On July 15, 1928, the group asked to "make manifest the love of God and man":

Another Christian mystic, Flower Newhouse was born Mildred Arlene Sechler on May 19 1909 in Pennsylvania. "Flower " was the name the young mystic insisted on being called as a child. Early in her childhood in Allentown PA, she demonstrated the gift of a well-trained clairvoyant. By six, she soon realized not everyone understood her gift. Once, when she shared her knowledge of the etheric realm with another six year-old. "Look " she said to the girl on the Staten Island Ferry, "See the water sprites!" Her traveling companion who saw only the blue-grey waters of Long Island Sound, thought Flower was imagining things. Flower, of course was shocked to find out what she witnessed did not exist for others. 7

Flower Newhouse continued to see water sprite, fairies, devas, and angels around her as an adult. Throughout her life, she demonstrated not only unique clairvoyance, but a mystic's love of Christ. Her special gift was seeing angels. Her angles, by the way, did not have wings; but appeared as perfected beings. She saw also huge angels usher in the dawn and follow the setting sun. She also saw angles at public events such as plays and musical performances. The angles were there to inspire the performers and uplift the audience. Eventually, Flower share more of her psychic gifts with the world . She wrote her first book in 1937 and added many other books and recordings until her death in 1994. In 1940 she founded a spiritual retreat, Questhaven, in Southern California.

In her book, *Kingdom of the Shining Ones*, she discussed the angels who serve Christ, truth, karma, and nature. She explained in the book that there are four waves of angels. The first is the "Nature Wave," the second, "the Life Motivation Wave," the third "the Wave of Divine Wisdom," and the fourth, "the Wave of Love."8 According to Flower Newhouse, angels by their invisible presence offer solace to a troubled heart, healing, and wisdom to those who pray.

In recent years, celebrities have become more public about their spiritual experiences, including Carlos Augusto Alves Santana. This Mexican and American musician who became famous in the late 1960s and early 1970s with his band, Santana and song Black Magic Woman Santana told Rolling Stone Magazine that he was an angel, Metatron who has been his guide since 1994. "Metatron is an angel. Santana has been in regular contact with him since 1994. Carlos will sit here facing the wall, the candles lit. He has a yellow legal pad at one side, ready for the communications that will come."9

Angels such as Metatron belong to a three-part a Divine hierarchy:

Supreme Hierarchy

Seraphim the highest choir of angels.

Cherubim the second highest in the nine hierarchies or choirs of angels. The Jews considered them as helpers of God.

Thrones Angels of pure Humility, Peace and Submission. They assist the lower choirs to contact God head.

Middle Hierarchy

Dominions Leaders who make known the commands of God.

Virtues The "shining ones" who watch over the seasons, stars, the sun and the moon. Often they bring miracles.

Powers Warrior Angels who defend against evil.

Lower Hierarchy

Archangels the most frequently mentioned throughout the Bible. Chief among them are the Archangels Michael, Gabriel and Raphael.

Angels Divine beings closest to the material world. They deliver prayer to God and can access the higher angels.

Angles have long been documented in near-death experiences such as that of Rev. Arthur Ford. In his 1952 book, *Why We Survive,* Ford described a profound near-death experience. The last thing that he heard as left his body was the doctor saying to the nurse, "Give him the needle. We might as well make him comfortable as there is nothing more we can do for him." Ford Drifted into unconsciousness with the thought "This is IT." 10

What happened next truly amazed the Spiritualist minister. He was surrounded on all sides by spirits of relatives and friends past. Those who had died in old age were younger, and those who had passed as babies were somehow grown up. As he went through the sea of faces, he became aware of a spiritual guide who led him though the fog to a beautiful landscape. "At some point (I had not consciousness of time) I found myself standing before a beautiful white building, a gleaming dazzling white such as I could never had imagined." 11 "This must be the Hall of Records", Ford thought when he was brought into a large room with two long tables with people sitting at them.

He was not surprised to find that they were talking about him. The spirit helpers guided him through a review of his life. "They knew about the selfish things that I had done years ago and like most people had pushed out of my conscious mind. They spoke of simple kindly things that every man does for others from time to time and promptly forgets. They obviously were trying to discover the main trend of my life."12 Ford heard the word "dissipation" several times, and realized that the guides were referring to lost opportunities. That seemed to be the real sin. According to Arthur Ford, "There was a plan for my life, and obviously, I had misread the blueprint."13

Ford had more work to do on earth. Before he knew it he was sent kicking and screaming back to the body he had so joyfully left on the hospital bed in Coral Gables, Florida. When he regained consciousness, he had more than a few choice words for the nurse in attendance. However, Arthur Ford fully recovered and shared his story of Divine intervention in *Why We Survive.* In the slim volume, Ford sums up what he learned from his near-death episode: "This had been a transforming experience for me. Fear had changed to faith founded on fact."14

In 1976, neuropathologist, Dr. George Rodonaia, underwent a life review during a near-death experience when he was hit by a car in 1976. According to Dr. Rodonaia, he found himself in a realm of total darkness."I had no physical pain, I was still somehow aware of my existence as George"15 Soon, he entered a world of constant brightness. According to Dr. Rodonaia "during this time the light just radiated a sense of peace and joy to me. It was very positive. I was so happy to be in the light. and I understood what the light meant. I learned that all physical rules for reality are nothing compared to this universal reality." 16

Next, Rodonaia underwent a life review which was similar in many ways to that of Rev. Arthur Ford.: "At some point, I underwent what has been called the 'life review process,' for I saw my life from beginning to end all at once , almost like a holographic image of my life going on before me--no sense of past, present or future, just now and the reality of my life." 17

Before his near-death experience, the doctor had been an atheist.. After his brush with death, Dr. Rodonaia decided to devote his lie to the study of religion and psychology. Now an ordained minister, Rev. Rodonaia feels that his NDE changed his life: "So I don't believe in the God of all Jews, or the Christians, or the Hindus, or in any one religions' idea of what God is or is not. It is all the same God, and that God showed me that the universe in which we live is a beautiful and marvelous mystery that is connected together forever and for always." 18

Anita Moorjani also became enlightened during her near-death experience which occurred in a comatose state February of 2006. The forty-seven year old woman was in the final throes of Stage IV cancer. All of her organs had shut down. In fact, the oncologist told her husband, Danny, that his wife had only hours left on earth. While Danny was praying for a miracle, his wife was aware of everything around her-- and felt no pain. Anita had drifted out of her body to the other side of life where she met her father who had died ten years before and her dearest friend, Soni, who had passed away two years before from cancer. She described heaven as a state more than a place: "It didn't feel as if I had *physically* gone somewhere else-- it was more as though I had *awakened*." 19 When Anita was given the choice of staying in this place of unconditional love or returning to her body which was now in a state of healing, she decided to return. Later, after she recovered fully from lymphoma, Anita Moorjani wrote about her near-death experience and subsequent miraculous return to health, *Dying To Be Me*. Her brush with death taught her two very important lessons-- to love herself unconditionally and to live fearlessly.

More recently, November of 2008, Dr. Eben Alexander III (born 1953) had a near death experience that transformed his life. The neurosurgeon who worked for 15 years at Brigham and Women's Hospital and Harvard Medical School went into a coma. His body was overcome by bacterial- induced meningitis. The condition was so severe that the doctors was given triple doses of antibiotics and placed on a ventilator in the Intensive Care Unit: During the seven days, he was in a coma, Alexander took a trip beyond the earth plane guided by an angel. He even met his departed relatives and a sister who had grown into a beautiful girl in a peasant dress .When Alexander recovered, he shared the life-changing event in his book, *Proof of Heaven.* According to Dr. Alexander his vivid and evidential near-death experience " proves that consciousness is independent of the brain, that death is an illusion, and that an eternity of perfect splendor awaits us beyond the grave-- complete with angels, clouds, and departed relatives." 20

End Notes

1 Holy Bible, Genesis 18.
2. Holy Bible, 2 ,Luke 1:26-28.
3. Holy Bible, John 20:12.
4. http://www.catholic.org/saints/saint.php?saint_id=295.
5. http://www.catholic.org/saints/saint.php?saint_id=295.
6. http://en.wikipedia.org/wiki/Angels_of_Mons.
7. http://en.wikipedia.org/wiki/Flower_A._Newhouse.
8. *Kingdom of the Shining Ones* , third edition,Christward Minister, 1955 Escondido CA, page 19.
9. "The Epic Life of Carlos Santana: Santana ", *Rolling Stone*, March 16, 2000.
10. Arthur A. Ford, *Why We Survive*, Gutenberg Press, Cooksburg NY, 1952, page 75.
11. Arthur A. Ford, *Why We Survive*, Gutenberg Press, Cooksburg NY, 1952, page 77.
12. Arthur A. Ford, *Why We Survive*, Gutenberg Press, Cooksburg NY, 1952, page 78.
13. Arthur A. Ford, *Why We Survive*, Gutenberg Press, Cooksburg NY, 1952, page 79.
14. Arthur A. Ford, *Why We Survive*, Gutenberg Press, Cooksburg NY, 1952, page 81.
15. http://www.ndef.org/ndef/NDE-Experiences/GeorgeRodonaia_nde.htm 16. http://www.ndef.org/ndef/NDE-Experiences/GeorgeRodonaia_nde.htm
17 http://www.near-death.com/experiences/evidence10.html
18. Anita Moorjani, Dying To Be Me, Hay H19. http://en.wikipedia.org/wiki/Eben_Alexander_(author).
20. http://en.wikipedia.org/wiki/Eben_Alexander_(author).

Chapter Eight:
Noted Astral Travelers

Trust the dreams, for in them is hidden the gate to eternity. **Khalil Gibran**

Hollywood is a Mecca for occultists, theosophists, and spiritualists. Going back to the days Rudolf Valentino, celebrities have been fascinated by the occult. Valentino and his wife, Natacha Rambova, were known to hold séance in the 1920s at Falcon Lair. Mae West, a Spiritualist, always made it a point to visit her favorite mediums, Jack Kelly, at Lily Dale Assembly. Some celebrities have even reported out of body experiences. Elizabeth Taylor, Sharon Stone, Eric Estrada, Jane Seymour and Peter Sellers to be precise. Both Elizabeth Taylor and Peter Sellers were in near-death states when the events occurred As Ms. Taylor explained to interviewer Larry King this happened in the late 50s. The British actress credits the spirit of her late husband for giving her the strength to go on with life. "I went to that tunnel, saw the white light, and Mike [Todd]. I said, 'Oh Mike, you're where I want to be.' And he said, 'No, Baby. You have to turn around and go back because there is something very important for you to do. You cannot give up now.' "1

Comic genius, Peter Sellers, had a similar experience. The star of Dr. Strangelove (1964) and the Pink Panther (1964), had his near-death experience after a series of heart attacks in 1964. According Shirley Sellers, he has felt himself leave his body and saw the doctor massages his heart below. Then Peter Sellers saw a radiant white light hovering above his body,and he had a strong desire to pass over. "I wanted to go to that white light more than anything. I've never wanted anything more. I know there was love, real love, on the other side of the light which was attracting me so much. Peter Sellers then heard a voice -- "It's not time. Go back and finish"2

Out of body experiences such as those of Peter Sellers and Elizabeth Taylor are frequently reported in near-death experiences. Many of the most prolific research on out of body has been done by notable scientists such as Emanuel Swedenborg (1747–65). who maintained a record of his out -of-body experiences in his Spiritual Diary. Swedenborg, by the way, carried a dream journal with him on most of his travels. He left a large volume of information on dreams and astral travel which was published in 1859 under the title Journal of Dreams. Swedenborg also possessed remarkable clairvoyant abilities. For instance, in July of 1759 he told his dinner party guests that there was a fire in Stockholm (405 km away) from his home. The report was later confirmed to be true.

Some noted astral travelers have even projected in the Great Pyramid of Giza. When explorer, Paul Brunton, had his mystical experience in the King's Chamber, he saw what he described as "monstrous elemental creations, evil horrors of the underworld.," then benevolent spirits of Egyptians priests." Apparently Bruton was out of his body during the mystical experience as he gazed down he saw his body lying prong attached by a silver cord of light. "He was given various information by his ancient guides, including the fact that the pyramid was built in the time of Atlantis, and that the Pyramid's secret chambers and ancient records were all contained within himself." 2

Brunton's experience of astral travel in the Great Pyramid is not unique. Joan Grant, Elisabeth Haitch and Earlyne Chaney all report past life memories as initiates in the Great Pyramid. Each has inhas recorded similar experiences as initiates.—Joan Grant in *Far Memory*, Elisabeth Haith, in *Initiation,* and Earlyne Chaney, *Initiation in the Great Pyramid.* According to Channey, after many years of training to become an initiate in her ancient Egyptian life, she was allowed to take the seven and final imitation in which all her past lives would be taken into account.

Her mentor, Anubis gave his advice:"He warned me of psychical enemies whose attacks must be prepared to repel. If I had preformed good works during my incarnations, the thought forms of those good works would now stand forth as my advocates shielding me from Apap, the dark serpent the devours the hidden light as the widening darkness of the autumn equinox devours the light of the year—Apap, the serpent of evil, the devourer of souls: Apap symbol of the animalistic body, as matter left mindless.3

The seventh and final initiation took three days. Earlyne made it through the fiery pit, to the Hall of Judgment, and finally through the star gate to Sirius to receive her final initiation. Here, she was reborn as a "Sun of God". On her return, "Earlyne" was awarded a golden Ankh to symbolize the soul's triumphant power over the cross of matter.

Edgar Cayce's guide also described the pyramids as places of initiation with the empty sarcophagus in the King's Chamber signifying there is no death. Cayce was an told by the Source that he had lived as the priest Ra Ta in ancient Egypt during the time of Nefertiti.. Dubbed " the Sleeping Prophet". Cayce retained his powers of astral travel in this life as well. As a medical clairvoyant he was able to enter a trance state and diagnose sick people thousands of miles away. He was even able to read the Book of Life: "Upon time and space written the thoughts, the deeds, the activities of an entity—as its relationships to its environs, its hereditary influences, as directed or judgment drawn by or according to what the entity's ideal is." 4 Cayce reported traveling astral to a library in which brown-robed monk handed him the life records of the person requesting a life reading.

Charles Webster Leadbeater was another prolific Western clairvoyant. When the Anglican priest discovered theosophy in 1883, he readily gave up the Anglican church, became a vegetarian and moved to Indian with the founder of theosophy, Madame Helena Blavatsky . In 1895, Leadbeater , with Annie Besant began an investigation of the occult nature of chemistry. Leadbeater turned out to be a remarkable clairvoyant with the ability to see the structure of the atom, which he diagrammed in his book, *Occult Chemistry*. Remarkably, scientists observed similar structures when microscopes were invented powerful enough to see into the atom!

Another author who sought to understand the esoteric nature of man was A. E. Powell. This theosophist wrote a series of books on the etheric, astral and causal bodies in the early 1900's A.E. Powell described the function of the astral body as follows "to make sensation possible, to serve as a bridge between the mind and the physical body, and to act as an independent vehicle of consciousness"2 This is especially true in dreams when he astral body functions independent of the physical. As Powel points out that the mental attitude can change the dream life: "Every impulse sent by the mind to the physical brain has to pass through the astral body, and as astral matter is far more responsive to thought vibrations than is physical matter, it follows that the effects produced on the astral body are correspondingly greater. Thus when a man has acquired mental control i.e. has learned to dominate the brain, to concentrate, to think. As and when he likes, a corresponding change will take place in his astral life; and if he brings the memory of that life through into the physical brain, his dreams will become vivid, well-sustained, rational and even instructive." 5

In the Twentieth Century, Hereward Carrington, Sylvan Muldoon and Robert Monroe have written extensively on astral travel. In 1929 the two coauthored a book, The Projection of the Astral Body. Carrington at that time was a well-known researcher who investigated séances and- psychics including greats as Mrs. Piper,- Eusapia Palladino,-Lizzie and May Bang and- Margery

Crandon. In 1927, Carrington was contacted by Sylvan Muldoon regarding a book Carrington had written astral projection. "Sylvan Muldoon (1903 –1971) had been experiencing astral travel since he was twelve, and was convinced anyone could do astral projectio. Muldoon and Carrington presented accounts of ordinary individuals who spontaneously left the body and safely returned. While Muldoon, had they had the ability to astral project at will, he believed most people did so naturally in their sleep. His technique for inducing out-of-body experiences included relaxation plus concentration on the pulse. Once one concentrated on the pulse to slow down the heart beat, attention is placed on the medulla oblongata (the back of the neck) .Like to ancient Egyptians, Muldoon believed the physical and astral bodies were connected by a silver cord of light:

A few years later, Oliver Fox wrote about his spontaneous astral travel. Oliver Fox was the pen name of Hugh George Callaway (1885–1949), a British author of short stories and poetry,. In 1939, he wrote an account of his dreams and astral travel experiences in *Astral Projection: A Record of Research.* In the book, he give accounts of places in the astral and those on each: At times the conditions seemed to be those prevailing physically at the time; at others he found himself enjoying warm sunshine in the middle of the night, or blue skies when it was physically raining outside. These travels, he concluded, were on the astral plane, while others were of an earthly location..6

In 1958, businessman, Robert Monroe began to have spontaneous out of the body experiences which he chronicled in a journal. Later, the journal was published under the title*: Journeys Out of the Body.* Sometimes the experience posed more questions than answers such as the time a mysterious intelligence entered without comment: "The intelligence force entered my head just above the forehead and offered no calming thoughts or words. It didn't seem to be aware of any of my feelings or emotions. It was looking impersonally, horridly and definitely for something specific in my mind. After a while (perhaps only moments, it left and I "reintegrated", arose shaken, and went outside for some fresh air. "7

In addition to communicating with mysterious forces Monroe visited friends in the astral state such as Dr. Bradshaw, made contact with the deceased and even experienced astral sex. He also made was given a book to read by a spiritual force. However he reports he was "too myopic" to see its pages clearly. As Monroe became familiar with different location she dubbed them simply Location I and Location II.

While most psychologists would term him delusional, Dr. Charles Tart, a parapsychologist, was intrigued by Monroe's experiences.. He even tested Robert Monroe with sophisticated equipment at the Electroencephalographic Laboratory at the University of Virginia from September 1965 to August 1966. Tart found that Monroe projected in a state very similar to dream Sleep. EEG tests at the University of Kansas Medical Center a decade later confirmed Tart's research.

Robert Monroe went on to found the Monroe Institute in Virginia, which continues to teach astral travel under the direction of his daughter, Laurie Monroe. The Monroe Institute utilizes a graded series of tapes which combine sound, music, guided imagery to induce out of body experience. The institute has patented a Hemi-Sync technology which persuade the two hemispheres of the brain to generate identical waves. The tapes are used to relax, heal, journey to the astral plane, as well as expand consciousness. Thousands, who have experienced one's Gateway Program, including the late Dr. Elisabeth Kubler-Ross attest to the success of the program. In one very moving session under the influence of "pink light" Dr Kubler-Ross, a pioneer in death and dying research, was greeted by the spirits of the many people she had helped through the change called death. 8

One noted participant Joseph McMoneagle, who also worked as a remote viewer at the Cognitive Research Laboratory at SRI International. CRL studied remote viewing from 1972 to 1995 under the direction of Dr. Hal Puthoff and Russell Targ and later Dr,. Edwin May. They were responsible for Project Stargate: an application of remote for military purposes. n December 28 1983, he was given these instructions by Robert Monroe: "Now you are at the library. Tell us something about the target in the envelope." The target was a slip of paper which said: "Who or what was Jesus and why was he here?" This was McMonealge' response to the query:

Joe: In the case of this manifestation, this man I am calling Christ. I t was to show that there is no such thing as fear… other than self-imposed creation. But… he did all of this in a very mystical way, though it originally wasn't meant to be. I sense history played a hand in the over-mystification of the message.9

In his book, *The Ultimate Time Machine*, McMoneagle went into the future. He predicted in 1998 that the world would be downsizing with significant restrictions on its citizens:"By 2010-2012 most Western countries will be suffering economically. American won't see relief until 2075-80." As for the stock, McMoneagle foresees a major drop in the market in 2006 due to war in the Mid East. Among his more positive predictions are new forms of high speed electromagnetic monorails being used and more control over teenagers with anti-gang legislation (2015) tracking devices for teens (2020), and immunization for teen against accidental pregnancy coming in 2050! 10

Another remote viewer, Skip Atwater studied at the Monroe Institute, He was U.S. Army Counterintelligence Special Agent. sent to the Monroe Insister to study astral l travel for the remote viewing intelligence program now known to world by the code name STAR GATE. He went into a sound-proof room and listened to instruction and music through a headphones. soon the bed began to raise and he had a plaint Roundy. Later, he asked Robert Monroe how he managed to lift the bed. To his surprise, Monroe explained that the cot was stationary. After several years of working at the Monroe Institute, Atwater *Captain of My Ship, Master of My Soul* which explored expanded states of consciousness.

Another well -known remote viewer is Ingo Swann. He became known for his work in remote viewing in 1972, when Director of Research American Society for Psychical Research Karlis Osis studied controlled out-of-body experiment with Swann. Later Swan along with Russell Targ, and Harold Puthoff created the military remote viewing program. According to Swann, Stanford Research International, had 95 to 85 % accuracy rate. However, Swan, an artist by profession became bored with viewing military target and requested something more interested. On the evening 27 April 1973 Targ and Puthoff gave Swann Jupiter as a target. They recorded Swann's remote viewing session of the Jupiter and Jupiter's moons. According to Swann: "Very high in the atmosphere there are crystals. they glitter. *Maybe* the stripes are like bands of crystals, *maybe* like rings of Saturn though not far out like that " 11 In 1979, the Voyager probe subsequently confirmed the existence of the rings.

End Notes

1. http://en.wikipedia.org/wiki/Emanuel_Swedenborg.
2. http://www.mysteriouspeople.com/Egyptian_Mystery.htm.
3. Earlyne Chaney, *Initiation in the Great Pyramid*, Astara Press, Upland, CA, page 175.
4. Edgar Cayce Reading 1651.
5. A. E. Powell, *The Astral Body*, The Theosophical Publishing House, Wheaton, ILL, 1927, page 95.
6. http://www.psywww.com/asc/obe/whois_fo.html.
7. Robert Monroe, *Journey Out of Body*, Broadway Books, New York, 1971, pages 260-261.
8. Source: Boyce Batey, President of Hartford, CT chapter of Spiritual Frontiers Fellowship.
9. Joseph McMoneagle, *The Ultimate Time Machine*, Hampton Road Publishing Company, Charlottesville, VA, page 8.
10. Joseph McMoneagle, *The Ultimate Time Machine*, Hampton Road Publishing Company, Charlottesville, VA, page 8.
11 http://en.wikipedia.org/wiki/Ingo_Swann.

Chapter Nine:
Techniques for Astral Travel

You may say that I am a dreamer, but I am not the only one. **John Lennon**

While Ingo Swann and Joseph McMoneagle preferred modern remote viewing skills, Eileen J. Garrett (1893-1970) honed her ability to do astral travel through her mediumship training. Remote viewing is in reality a form of controlled clairvoyance. For example, in 1932, Eileen Garrett participated in a an experiment with scientist to astral travel to a target in Newfoundland. She correctly gave description other room, even the exact words of the conversation taking place in Newfoundland to the note-taker in New York City: I could see objects on the table not by ordinary sight but through clairvoyant vision; I gave a description of what I saw to the note-taker in New York. I heard the doctor say 'make apologies to the experimenters at you rend. I have head an accident and cannot work as well as I had hoped.'"1 Mrs. Garrett even went on to describe the bandage on the doctor's had which was later to be confirmed to be true.

In her book *Awareness,* Eileen Garrett give excellent tips on developing psychic skills, including "traveling clairvoyance". Sylvan Muldoon, William Bulhman, Sean David Morton, Scott Rogo and Waldo Vieira also have added much to the literature on astral travel. Robert Monroe used guided imagery and a technique called semi-sync, some remote viewers, on the other hand, insist on a strict protocol for their research.

What does science have to say about all this? One of the first scientists to investigate astral travel was Dr. Robert Crookall. He examined over 750 cases of astral travel and found convincing evidence of their validity. In 1960, he published The Study and Practice of Astral Projection. He found most subjects left through the top of their head and momentarily blacked out for a second as they left the body and returned .A another interesting fact found was subject felt jolted when the astral body returned too quickly.

By measuring brain waves, science has found that there are varying levels of consciousness from waking Beta state to light hypnotic trance of Alpha to deep trance state of Theta to unconscious Delta state. The mind , apparently never really ceases to function--only varies in levels of functioning.

States of Consciousness

Beta (13+ cycles per second) waking state, active consciousness, affirmations

Alpha (8 to 12 cycles per second) daydreaming, meditation, light trance, light hypnosis

Theta (5 to 7 cycles per second) deep trance, deep hypnosis, deep trance

Delta (5 to 4 cycles per second) Unconscious (For those who are trained to maintain consciousness lucid dreaming and astral travel)

Sylvan Muldoon, one of the first to research astral projection, concurred with ancient Egyptian literature. He believed as did the ancient Egyptians, that the physical and astral bodies were connected by a silver cord of light: "My two identical bodies were joined by an elastic-like cable which was fastened to the medulla oblongata. region of the astral counterpart, while the other centered between the eyes of the physical counterpart." When the mental beat and heart beat become in sync, the silver cord of light can loosen to allow the astral body leave the body at will. Muldoon did not recommend his method for those with heart conditions.

Later, author Robert Bruce expanded on this concept in his book, Astral Dynamics. Bruce felt that through astral projection, a person could travel to higher and more subtle plans of existence. This mystical approach is similar to that of the Hindus. It has been replaced by the more scientific model of Robert Monroe, the Virginia businessman was surprised by his spontaneous out-of the body experiences which occurred in 1958. He began a journal to help understand what was happening to his body. Later, the journal became the classic, *Journeys Out of the Body*. Here is his entry for September 9th, 1960: "I was lying in a north-south position, when I suddenly felt bathed in and transfixed b a very powerful beam that seemed to come from the north about 30 degrees above the horizon. It had intelligence in a form beyond my comprehension and it came directly (down the beam)into my head and seemed to be searching every memory in my mind.2

Naturally, these experience disturbed Monroe. Try as he might he could not explain what was happening to him Soon he was communicating not only with mysterious forces, but also was visiting friends in the astral state such as Dr. Bradshaw, made contact with the deceased and even experienced astral sex. He also made was given a book to read by a spiritual force. However he reports he was "too myopic" to see its pages Clearly. As Monroe became familiar with different locations, he dubbed them simply Location I and Location II.

While most psychologists would term him delusional, Dr. Charles Tart, a parapsychologist was intrigued by Monroe's experiences. He even tested Robert Monroe with sophisticated equipment at the Electroencephalographic Laboratory at the University of Virginia from September 1965 to August 1966. Tart found that Monroe projected in a state very similar to dream sleep. EEG tests at the University of Kansas Medical Center a decade later confirmed Tart's research.

How did Robert Monroe manage to project in the dream state? Monroe used three factors to successfully astral travel. First, self-hypnosis to achieve a relaxed state of sleep. Next affirmation such "I will recall every detail in this state of relaxation" Then he advised the mediator to lie with his head to magnetic north in a quiet totally dark room in comfortable loose clothing. When you are ready, give yourself the mental suggestion to remember the session. With practice, most people can achieve a state bordering sleep or the hypnologic state which Monroe termed Condition A. Next, it is necessary to clear the mind by ignoring and mental discharges, Condition B. Then the mediator can achieve a state without body sensation Condition C. Finally the person enters a void , where vibrations begin. At this point Monroe advised separating from the physical body by concentrating the blackness in front about three feet away, then six feet away. "Hold for awhile until the point is firmly established. From there turn the point 90 degrees upward on a line parallel to the body axis and reaching out above the head. Reach for the vibration at that spot. " 3

In 2000, one of Monroe's students, Joseph MecMoneagle, published a handbook on remote viewing: *Remote Viewing Secrets.* His method was to train subjects through a series of exercises progressing from simple to more complex targets. McMoneagle's method, similar to Project Stargate used by the military to train remote views insists on strict scientific protocol. He recommended that people do their remote viewing "totally blind to the target," and to keep a notebook with your thoughts and methods of "cognitive processing. He stressed the importance of starting with the large image and working your way to details: "Initially try and stick with major gestalts, slowly working your way into more detail. Open to whatever your subconscious wants to share with you, when it want to share it." 4.

These suggestions along with a sense of humor, plus the realization that "learning process never stops" listed as "good practices" McMoneagle's research also uncovered an interesting difference between male and female remote views. Men in the study were more apt to draw the target, while women were more apt to verbally describe it.

Clairvoyant and psychic investigator, Dr. Douglas Baker, has taken a more esoteric approach to astral projection. Baker is both a seer with spirit guides such as Master Robert Browning and a medical doctor. He was born in Britain and raised in South Africa, and later returned to England. He has done extensive research on astral travel as well as esoteric anatomy , esoteric healing, esoteric anatomy, esoteric astrology, and esoteric psychology. As a medical advisor to the De La Warr Laboratories in Oxford, England, Dr. Baker did research on radionics and biomagnetism. In the 1970s, he established Claregate College, a correspondence college.

Dr. Baker has also written a book on astral travel: *Practical Techniques of Astral Projection.* His previous research into the Akashic Records through astral projection is well documented. Guided at times by the spirit of Master Robert Browning, he believes in the importance of will."Projection being basically astral or emotional in nature requires strong DESIRE FACTOR to be present" 5 Dr. Baker in his book, *Practical Techniques of Astral Travel* suggests projecting a few feet out of the body and then farther out. He believes a strong desire to reach the target combined with visualization and, of course, practice will being results. He also suggests deep breathing to facilitate the process.

Another remote viewer Sean David Morton also advocates a more spiritual approach to remote viewing. Sean David Morton, a student of Tibet Buddhism taught workshops in Spiritual Remote Viewing. According to Morton "Astral travel without a spiritual guide is like rubbing yourself with barbeque sauces and running naked through the woods." It is no wonder then that Morton's Spiritual Remote Viewing program incorporates Tibetan chants and meditation with modern remote viewing techniques developed by Russell Targ at Stanford Research Institute. After a run-down on meditation and Tibetan chants for protection, the student is guided to "read" the contents of three envelopes. Later, students are encouraged to visualize a space ship to take them across a bridge to a selected remote viewing location.

William Buhlman's methods for out-of body travel fall somewhere between the military protocol of McMoneagle and the spiritual approach of Morton. His description of out of body parallels Monroe's In his book, *Adventures Beyond the Body,* Bulhman gives this description of the separation process: "The sensations during separation were normally similar, a buzzing sound accompanied by an internal high-energy or vibration feeling spreading through my body. At the peak of vibrations, I would mentally direct myself away from my body by sitting up or rolling out of my body."6

Once out of his body, Buhlman devised a series of commands to gain control. He also found out that it was important to be precise about what he asked for. In his 1996 book Adventures Out of the Body, he advised shouting out "Control now!" or "Clarity now!. Using these command, he was able to control his mind in a concrete manner.

Buhlman's out- of -body experiments began with simple trips to visit his mother's home to trying to move a pencil in the astral state (which he did after many tries). Soon his journeys took him beyond the everyday to a meeting with the spirit of his Uncle Willie and even a vivid past life recall of a life as a Tibetan monk who was murdered by the Chinese. The benefits of out-of-body travel according to Buhlman range from relaxation, to spontaneous healing, increased knowledge, intuition, proof of immortality and past life recall.

Other researches such as Brazil's Waldo Vieira(1932) would d agree. Dr. Vieria, a dentist, has had out of body experience since age nine. Vieira argues that consciousness can exist beyond the body. For 40 years he has studied parapsychology and experiences of out of body journeys which he believes prove an existence independent form the body. He founded the International Institute of Projectiology and Conscienciology for the purpose of systematic study of astral projection. Dr. Vieira has also published his many out of body experiences in his book, *Projections of Consciousness*. He often received visits from the spirit world, including one touching encounter with the spirit of his mother, Aristina on September 9, 1979: Vieira could see his mother's face clearly and commented " You are younger and more beautiful." 7

In conclusion, there are many views on astral projection, ranging from being guided by spirit to purely mechanical techniques. Take a look at the seven techniques listed at the end of the chapter. Choose one and practice it faithfully for twenty-eight day. Then record your results.

Dream Journal III

Since astral travel is natural dream function, take time to remember your dreams in a dream journal. As you record dreams, underscore those in which you are flying, visiting familiar places or other countries. Give yourself the suggestion before you go to sleep: "Astral travel is a natural state. I can easily travel in my sleep. I will remember my journeys in vivid detail when I awake." Be sure to date each dream and underline the names of people, places, and significant events.

Candle Meditation

Start with a prayer of protection such as The Lord's Prayer. Surround yourself with white light and call on Infinite Intelligence or God for protection Sit in a chair in a comfortable position with feet on the floor.. A chair with arms or a recliner is usually the best. Place a candle on a table opposite you at eye level, about 18 inches away. Light the candle and gaze steadily into the flames for 30 seconds . When you are ready, close your eyes and allow your mind's eye to follow the after image . Hold the image in your third eye as long as you can. Allow your consciousness to remain steady, focusing on the after image of the flame. With practice the flame can open a portal to the other side. You will know you are on the other side when you see a group of faces. Go beyond the sea of faces, and allow your consciousness to travel to the higher mental planes.

Witch's Cradle

Try swinging in a witch's cradle. First construct the cradle as follows: Use a large sack made of loosely woven material. Make sure the sack is strong enough to support you and not air tight. Suspend the cradle over a beam. The cradle should be suspended about a foot off the ground. Have a friend spin you in it for a few minutes. The gentle rocking is disorienting and simulates astral projection.

Witch often used this technique at night in isolated places. The initial disorientation, the quiet and the darkness are forms of sensory deprivation which has been known to stimulate out-of-body experiences. Try swinging for three minutes and gradually work up to ten minutes. Record your results.

Target Technique

Choose an object that you can readily visualize. For example a object from your home. Visualize the object and examine it in your mind's eye. Then begin to create a strong desire to be with that object. Before going to sleep visualize that object and give yourself the suggestion you will visit the object in your sleep.

For example if you have special item such as a bust of Nefertiti that sits on a file cabinet in library of your home, try to reach to object . Once you see Nefertiti, you can look around the library and other rooms of your home. With practice, a student can start to project to more exotic places such as the Great Pyramid at Giza

Jane Roberts who channeled Seth used to put a picture up weekly in her office for students use as a target. Try the same exercise with a friend. Have a friend put a picture up in a space in their home with which you are familiar. Alternately an object may be put out for you to astral-view. Before sleep, also give yourself the suggestion to visit and view the object. With practice, students begin to see the colors, shapes or words in the picture.

Guided Imagery Exercise

Stretch your right foot out, then relax, Next stretch your left foot out, and relax . Make a fist with your right hand, then relax. Make a fist with your left hand, then relax. Now hold your stomach in for a count of seven, then relax completely. Roll your head slowly to the right, then slowly to the left. Take seven deep breaths in through the nose, out through the mouth.

Imagine yourself in yourself in a hot-air ballon.. See yourself rising higher and higher in the balloon. You are seated in the pilot's chair with a set of controls in front of you. Take a moment to decide where you would like to visit. Relax and set sail. At the count of five, but not before, you wil see a bridge in front of you. This is not an ordinary bridge. It is a bridge which takes you across time and space to the target location. One, just relax your body. Two, breathe deep. Three, you are happy to return. Four, you are almost there. Five, see the bridge in front of you. You are getting closer and closer. You are now floating effortless over the bridge of time and space. As you go across this bridge, you see in front of you a clear view of your destination. Slowly land your balloon and open the door. As you step outside, you feel free and peaceful. Walk around the place. Pay attention to details.

Play soft music such Kitaro's Silk Road for three minutes.

Now you are ready to return. You will remember all details. By the count of five, but not before you will return. One you are now entering your hot-air balloon. Two, see yourself gently lifting off. Three, you are crossing the time bridge. Four you are going back home. Five, eyes wide open. You are back.

Into the Future Exercise

Try this exercise to remote view the future. Sit or lie in a comfortable position. Then take three deep breaths in through the nose, out though the mouth Relax. See yourself going down a long white corridor into the future. As you walk down the hall you are going five years into the future:

One. You have the ability absolutely to project into the future.

Two. You have a strong desire to see the future.

Three. You are protected with white light and wisdom.

Four. You are going one, two, year, four five years ahead in time.

Five You are now in the year (date fives from now)

Imagine yourself at the table having your morning beverage. Visualize the kitchen or dining area clearly. You feel rested, Well, and peaceful. As you look around the table, you spy a folded newspaper, The New York Times (or the name of the daily news in your community.) Bring the paper so it exactly in front of you.

On the count of three, but not before , you will open the newspaper and be able to read the headlines for ________(future date).

One, you have the paper in your hands.

Two you are ready to open it.

Three, open it and read the headlines.

What does it say? Take your time. Now look at the front page. Are there any pictures? If so, describe them. Look around the front and read carefully the articles there. Take your time. You will remember all details when you return. Is there any other interesting news? If so turn that page and read about it. Take a minutes to read the paper.

When you are ready, close the paper and relax. See yourself walking onto a long white corridor back to present time. Time

You are Ready to return.

Two you will remember all details.

Three, you are rested.

Four you are beginning to awake.

Five, eyes wide open back to ______today's date

End Notes

1. H. F. Provost Battersby , *Man Outside Himself,* University Books, Inc, New York, NY.
2. Robert Monroe, *Journey Out of Body*, Broadway Books, New York, 1971, pages 260-261.
3. Robert Monroe, *Journey Out of Body,* Broadway Books, New York, 1971, page 213.
4. Joseph McMoneagle, *The Ultimate Time Machine*, Hampton Road Publishing Company, Chalottesville, VA, page 118.
5. Dr. Douglas Baker, *Practical Techniques of Astral Projection*, Aquarian Press, Wellingborough, England, page 39.
6. William Buhlman, *Adventures Beyond the Body*, Harper-Collins Publishers, New York, 1996, page 26.
7. Dr. Waldo Vieira, Projections of the Consciousness, International Academy of Consciousness, London, 2007, page 80.

Chapter Ten:
Traveling the Time Lines

When the iron eagle flies and horses run on wheels, the Tibetan people will be scattered over the earth, and the dharma will go to the land of the Red Man (the West). ***Padmasambhava*** *8th century AD*

Astral travel is a very real event in Tibetan monasteries. For thousands of years, Tibetan monks have been traveling the time lines. Tibetan lamas can even to go back in time to view an initiate's past lives or forward in the future for divination. California psychic, Sean David Morton, was awed by the dedication and skill of Tibetan lamas during an eight- month stay in India. In 1986: he had a \ life-changing meeting with the Dalai Lama. The Dalai Lama told Morton to travel to the T'ang Boyche monastery in Nepal. When he arrived there in late May, Lama Rinpochi Lopsang Tundun recognized Morton as a monk who had lived in the monastery in past life. The high priest brought the young man down to the basement where he took a top off a dusty box to reveal a robe and other possessions that were saved by the monks in anticipation of his return. Apparently, Morton who was born in 1956, was an incarnation of a Tibetan monk killed by Chinese soldiers in 1953! 1

Tragically, over 6,000 monasteries in Tibet, were ransacked and destroyed by the Chinese Communists during their take-over.in the late 1940s and 1950s. Some of the more advanced lamas used their psychic powers to simply exit their bodies. Lama Yeshe and Lama Zope even described how some monks captured by the Red Chinese left their bodies at will. The imprisoned monks and nuns reported "the remarkable sight of lamas quietly retiring to a corner of their cells, taking up meditation position, and, without further ado, simply leaving their bodies. They were neither sick nor dying, but were practicing powa, the transformation of consciousness to a different existence. Apparently hundreds practiced powa at this grim time." 2 Some adepts in the country side were even rumored to achieve the Rainbow body or to ascend taking their physical body with them.

According to Tibetan tradition, attaining the "rainbow body" by releasing the physical body to the five elements is the highest attainment of yogin.Togen Ugyen Tenzin ,a Tibetan master who imprisoned by the Chinese died in this manner. When Tendzin's spirit left the body, only his sheepskin robe still standing upright was left behind. No trace of his body was found.

Togden, by the way, was a skilled in dream divination. When Togden's deceased lama, Drugpa Rinpoche was ready to incarnate, Togden had a dream in which he met the deceased lama in the house of Nozang family. A year later, as predicted, a baby boy was born in into the family. 3 He was also was an excellent clairvoyant. However he was sometimes sadden to "see" the evil thought of others. . He decided to shut down his clairvoyance by drinking the" the urine of a widow" deliberately to rid himself of this hindrance to compassion.4

How do Tibetan lamas achieve these miraculous powers or siddhis? It is through raising their spiritual awakening. Each individual possesses the sacred kundalini energy at the base of his or her spine. As one evolves spiritually, beyond the lower centers of materialism, sensuality, and ego, the heart center is filled with compassion. Eventually the gifts of the three higher centers clairaudience, clairvoyance and Cosmic consciousness unfold. However, opening the siddhis is rare, and not always possible for millions who practice spiritual disciplines. According to kundalini expert, Gopi Krishna, "in almost all cases of genius and psychic powers, the gift in born, being part of the natural mental endowment of the human being."5 .It is extraordinary that psychic gifts are cultivated to advanced degree demonstrated by trained Tibetan seers.

Several factors may be at work. First, young men who are drawn to religious life may have already cultivated siddhis from past lives which would give them a strong impetus for mental development in the present life. Also, monks must take vows of renunciation which are designed to close the lower centers. To begin with, monks must adhere to the Five e Precepts:

1. I undertake to abstain from harming living beings.
2. I undertake to abstain from taking what is not given .
3. I undertake to abstain from sexual misconduct.
4. I undertake to abstain from false speech.
5. I undertake to abstain from intoxicating drugs or drink.

The second factor is withdrawal from the outer world. As monks separate from the world, they learn to focus their energy inward for the purpose of enlightenment. They practice both outward renunciation as well of inward renunciation. Young monks are taught to practice the triple gem consisting of devotion Buddha, dedication to dharma and sangha, or spiritual community. They are admonished not to fall back to the t lower realms of material desires and pride which separate one from God consciousness and could lead to a lower existence in their next lifetime.

Virtuous acts in this life are rewarded in the next incarnation. For this reason, it is important to avoid all harmful acts and to forsake the company of irreligious people. Following the example of the Buddha, monks are required to remain even tempered and to aid others regardless of what others have done to them. Stealing, lying, sexual misconduct and ill-will will cause one to take a lower birth, while virtuous karma results in greater opportunities in this life and the next.

Tibetan Buddhists view their ultimate goal as liberation of all living beings. Meditation plays a central role in their spiritual practice. Initiates use a wide variety of objects for mental concentration. One method of the Tibetan Buddhist tradition is to focus on an image of the Buddha. Once the statue of Buddha is familiar than they close their eyes and focus on the image in their imagination. The monks are also taught to chant scared chants and to focus on the breath as means of calming the mind

Citing laziness and procrastination as barriers to the practice of meditation, first-year monks are urged to remain enthusiastic and dedicated to mediation. It is important to remember the instruction for proper meditation, as well as have a calm, but enthusiastic attitude. The mind should be free of agitation, yet not dull or sleepy. With sincere and regular practice the monk will experience higher consciousness.

In addition to meditation, service is emphasized. Giving material aid should be done in an attitude of non-attachment: "One should give not with the intention of making others serve one, but in order to afford them the opportunity to attain a higher level of existence in the next life, nirvana or enlightenment." 6 Giving encouragement to others is also important" One should speak with others at their own intellectual level, giving them teachings that can best be used by them. Next, comes teaching others spiritual practices. Finally monks are admonished to become examples of the spiritual teaching. Setting an example is the powerful way to teach, for one cannot successfully teach others what you have not mastered.

One of the most fascinating practices of the monks is called "tumo" or psychic heat which arises spontaneously during religious experiences to keep the adept physically warm. One of the first Westerners to observe this practice was Alexandra David-Neel. She was born Louise Eugénie Alexandrine Marie David in France in 1868. She visited Tibet In 1924 when it was still forbidden to foreigners. David-Neel was received by the Dali Lama, and spent time in Tibetan occult centers where she observed psychic rites during her 14 years in the " Land of the Snow." Her unique experiences with psychic phenomena such as tumo and thought projection were chronicled in her book, *The Magic and Mystery of Tibet* Jack Kerouac and Allen Ginsberg, philosopher Alan Watts were all influenced by her teachings.

According to Madame David-Neel, Tibetan gurus are known for their powers of telepathy: "There exist men today who affirm they have beheld visions transmitted to them by a kind of telepathic process... Sometimes the vision papers during period of mediation, but at other times it is seen while the observer is busy with his ordinary affairs." 8 These visions are quite different from those seen in a dream.

In *The Magic and Mystery of Tibet* " To spend the winter in a cave amidst the snows , at altitude that varies between 11,000 and 18,000 feet, clad in a thin garment, even naked, and escape freezing is a somewhat difficult achievement. Yet numbers of Tibetan hermits go safely each year through this ordeal" 7 The Tibetan adept have mastered the art of "tumo" "In the secret teaching, tumo is also the subtle fire which warms the generative fluid and drives the energy in it, till it runs all over the body along the tiny channels of "the rtsa" (veins artery or nerve)"9

According to J.H. Brennan, there are three types of tumo. The first type is spontaneous. The second type of tumo arises from mystical experiences. "The third type of tumo is related to the subtle fire that warms the seminal fluid in a man and is the source of its energy. When the warmth is heightened, the energy runs throughout energy channels of the body." Tumo may also be achieved by visualizing a deity or though breath practice.10 With these powerful techniques, Tibetan monks often see far into the future. Here is the testimony of a monk astral projecting in 1967 to the year 2012: "He saw Russia and China 'settle their differences' around 2008. After that 'people from outer space' would come to demonstrate peace. The Tibetan was hopeful for civilization beyond 2012 when People will learn the essence of spirituality, the relation between body and the soul, the reincarnation and the fact we are connected with each other are all part of "God" 11

Five Tibetan Exercises

While it is necessary to study with a master teacher to learn time travel, much of the preliminary work can be done through meditation, spiritual reading and practicing the Five Tibetan Exercises which originated in the Himalayas. These exercises were brought to the West in the early 20th century by a retired British army officer who received them from a teacher in a Tibetan lamasery. Regular practice of these five postures will strengthen the body, improve concentration and energize the chakras. Be sure to check with your physician if you have any back or health problems before you begin the **Five Tibetan Exercises**. For the first week do each exercise once. The second week, do each exercise three times. Then gradually over the course of the next month increase your repetition to 21 times.

Exercise One: Twirling from Left to Right

Stand with your arms outstretched from the shoulder. Keep both arms rigid as you spin from left to right (clockwise) seven times or until you become dizzy. With practice you may increase your spins gradually to 21 gentle spins.

Exercise Two: Leg Lift

Lie on the floor with arms at your side. Keep both legs together and slowly raise them up and let your feet extend over your body if comfortable.. You may wish to raise your head a bit as you perform the leg lift. Do not bend your knees. Hold this position for a few seconds then slowly lower the feet to the floor. Lower the head as well. Relax Exercise may be repeated several times if you so desire.

Exercise Three: Backward Bend

Kneel on the floor with hands at you side. Keep your chin on your chest, lean backward as far as comfortable. As you arch your back, curl your toes and place your arms and hands on your thighs for support.

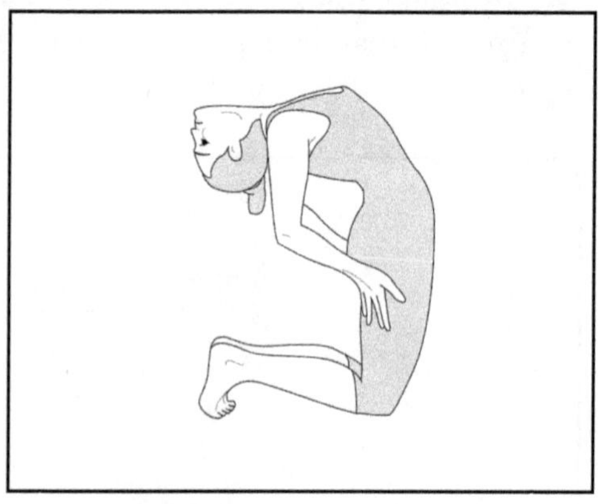

Exercise Four: Pelvic Lift

Lie on the floor with your knees bent, feet flat, and palms down. When you are ready , gently lift y our pelvis about 8 inches off the floor. Hold for ten seconds. Slowly lower your pelvis back to the floor.

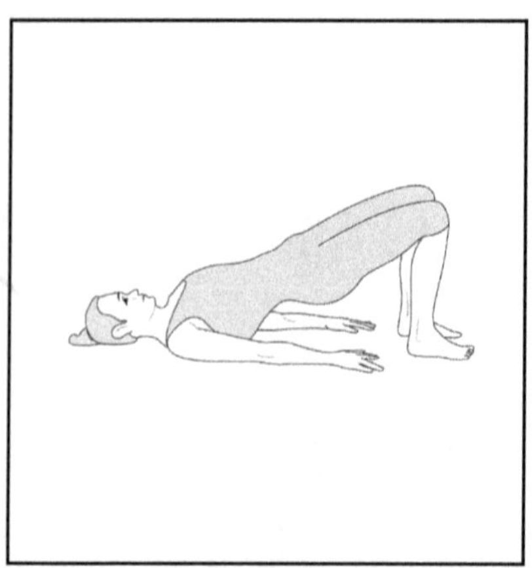

Exercise Five, Part one A

Lie down on your stomach. Flex your toes and place hand down o the floor. Gently raise your chest up into a sagging position. Throw your head back. This is similar to the locust position in yoga. Hold this position for 20 seconds.

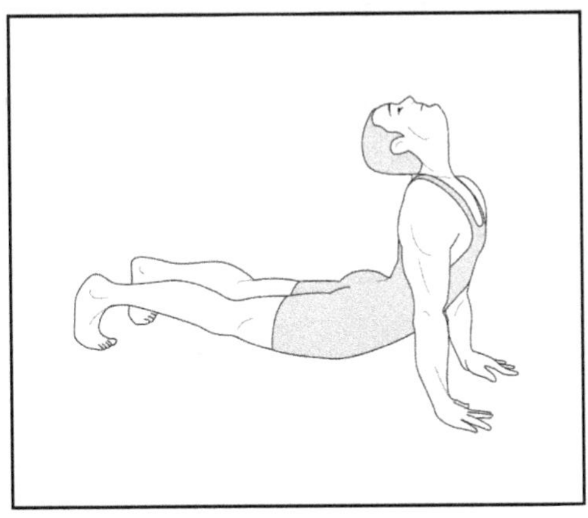

Exercise V, Part B

Then bending at the hips bring your body up to an inverted V position. Tuck your chin into the chest. Hold for a few seconds. This position is similar to the "downward dog position in yoga.

Once you have completed the exercises, you may wish to meditate. Spread a mat on the floor and assume the "corpse" pose. Just lie down on the floor, flat on your back, arms and legs are spread at a 45 degree angle. Focus on your breathing. Feel the abdomen rise and fall with each breath. Scan your body for any signs of tension. Let the tension go, as you gently focus on your breath for ten minutes of quiet meditation. The benefits of the corpse pose are many: lower blood pressure, decrease in anxiety, increase in energy, deeper sleep, more productivity, and improved self esteem.

End Notes

1 http://en.wikipedia.org/wiki/Sean_Morton.

2. Vickie Mackenzie, *Born in the West*, Marlowe & Company, New York, 1996, page 7.
3. Chogyal Namkhai Norbu, *Rainbow Body*. North Atlantic Books, Berkeley CA, 2012, pages R 35-36 .
4. Chogyal Namkhai Norbu, *Rainbow Body*. North Atlantic Books, Berkeley CA, 2012, page 46.
5. Krishna, Gopi, Kundalini, the Evolutionary Energy in Man, Bolder Colorado, Shaballa Publications, 1967.
6. Geshe Ngawang Dhargyeye, *Tibetan Tradition of Mental Development* , Library of Tibetan Works and Archive, second edition, 2003, page 161.
7. Alexandra David-Neel, *Magic and Mystery in Tibet*, Dover Publications, New York, NY, 1971, page 216.
8. Alexandra David-Neel, *Magic and Mystery in Tibet*, Dover Publications, New York, NY, 1971, page 240.
9. Alexandra David-Neel, *Magic and Mystery in Tibet*, Dover Publications, New York, NY, 1971, page 217.
10. http://www.lifepositive.com/Spirit/world-religions/buddhism/tumo.asp.
11. http://www.in5d.com/1967-tibetan-monk-astral-travels-to-2012.html.

Chapter Eleven:
Past Life Memories

Our birth is but a sleep and a forgetting
The soul that rises with us, our life's star
Has elsewhere its setting
And cometh from afar.

Wordsworth

Astral travel takes the dreamer into the past as well as the future. As the poet William Wordsworth wrote the soul "cometh from afar." For the majority of the world population who believe in reincarnation "afar" means a past life. According to French philosopher, Voltaire "It is not more surprising to be borne than twice than once ." Two thirds of the world's population --Buddhist and Hindus believe in reincarnation Chief among the Westerners who would agree with Voltaire are Napoleon Bonaparte, William Wordsworth, Louisa May Alcott, Richard Wagner, Henry Ford, General George Patton, and Princess Diana. While Napoleon believed he was an incarnation of Charlemagne, General Patton recalled many scenes of Roman battles. Princess Diana, on the other hand, believed she had been a nun in another life.

Dreams, as well as astral travel can be a rich source of past life remembrance. While many dreamers who spontaneously see themselves in old-fashioned dress pass it off to imagination, if they looked closely they would see the face of a slightly different version of themselves in the garb of the day. For instance, ten-year old dreamer, Nancy, saw herself as an old woman in a long dress and a pioneer bonnet walking down the hill with a heavy oak bucket to fetch water. As she reached the well, she felt a jolt go through her body and her physical body went backward, while her energy body instantaneously moved forward at the point of death. Why did the child have this dream? It was because Nancy went to sleep afraid she might die because of severe pains in her stomach. Far from frightening the child, the dream was comforting, letting her know there is no death. Also, as she experienced this knowledge, her stomach ache went away as well!

Past life dreams such as Nancy's occur because of a current situation that has its source in a past life. These past live remembrance can be very helpful in the present life, and more journalists such Michael Schmicker, author of *Best Evidence,* are beginning to take reports of past lives more seriously. Take the case of Doris Williams, an RN from Ohio, who had a life-long fear of small boats and deep water. Under hypnosis she recalled a life as Stephen Blackwell, a clerk who perished on the Titanic. Michael Schmicker reviewed the evidence and states Stephen Blackwell was listed Walter Lord's *A Night to Remember*, and many of the details Doris Williams provided under hypnosis rang true. Even little-known facts such as being emplyed by the Brown company checked out: "A review of a half-century old U.S. Senate investigative report on the disaster confirmed that Stephen Blackwell had indeed been employed by Brown Shipley (not " Shipping") Company, once located at the address she remembered. Blackwell Age 43 had been returning to America from a business trip to England when the Titanic sank. " 1 It is intriguing to note, that Doris Williams lost some of her fear of water and small boats; however, she had no desire to do any more past life regressions.

Many psychologists, such as the late Dr. Arthur Guirdham have found idea of reincarnation worthy of study. He investigated an usual case of a woman, Mrs. Smith" who recalled her life in southern France as a Cathar in the thirteenth century. The Cathars were considered so extreme in their belief in reincarnation, that a crusade was ordered against them,. They would rather starve, a form passive suicide than give up their beliefs. Guirdham's book *The Cathars and Reincarnation* recounts many details of Mrs. Smith of life as a Cathar including drawings of old coins, jewelry and names . In nightmares she recalled being burned at the stake in the dream state. She also gave details about the Cathars that only recently were able to be confirmed. For example, Mrs. Smith always maintained that the Cathar priests wore dark-blue vestaments, contrary to the belief by historian that the priests only wore black; "For twenty-six years including six years correspondence with me, she (Mrs. Smith) stubbornly maintained they wore dark blue." She was proved correct by Jean Duvernoy of Toulouse but only in the last four years . In editing the registrar of Jacques Fournier, Monsieur Duvernoy revealed Cathar priests sometimes wore dark blue or dark green. Since the book was published in 1965, there was no way Mrs. Smith who had these dreams beginning in 1944 could have gained the information from Duvernoy's book."2

Other psychologists who have written book includes, the late Dr. Helen Waumback, Dr. Edith Fiori, and Dr. Brian Weiss. Dr. Bruce Goldberg, a dentist turn hypnotherapist, is one of the foremost experts in the field of past life regression. One of the most detailed cases of past life regression was chronicled in Goldberg's *A Search for Grace*. Dr. Bruce Goldberg, a dentist turned hypnotherapist, regressed a young woman trapped in a "on again-off again" relationship with her abusive boyfriend. Apparently, Ivy, had a lot to learn! Under hypnosis, she recalled a lifetime as a 1920's party girl in Buffalo, New York. Her name was Grace Doze. In that lifetime, Grace had an affair with another man while married to Chester Doze. The affair ended with her murder by her lover, Jake, who incidentally incarnated as her abusive boyfriend in this life as well! Fortunately, Ivy was able to let go of her abusive relationship in this life.

What made the case so remarkable was Dr. Goldberg's research. He was able to locate articles from *the Buffalo Courier*, May 1927, which corroborated Ivy's life as Grace Doze. The articles also confirmed the information given under hypnosis listing Grace date of death, manner of death (strangling), and the names of her husband, mother and son, as well as their addresses.

The question naturally arises, "What happens when one doesn't forget a past life?" Why do some such as Jenny Cockell remember past lives. Born in 1953 in England, young Jenny began to have memories of a life as a young mother in Ireland. She remember her name—Mary Sutton and that of her husband--John Sutton, as well as the names of her young children. When "Mary" died October 24, 1932, a month after her last child was born, she left this world with the thought "What would become of my motherless brood with only an alcoholic father to watch over them?".

It was a question that was to haunt Mary Sutton when she returned 21 years later as Jenny Cockell. As Jenny grew up she became obsessed by dreams of Ireland and sought out answers. She turned to past life regression. Under past life regression, she learned more details about the cottage in Malahideher, her husband, as well as the names of four of her eight children in that life: "Under hypnosis four of the children were given names, but my response to the questions were so casual that I had many doubts about these names--James, Mary, Harry, and Kathy. -as I did about Mary's husband's name. The dead baby boy whom I saw under hypnosis only . was, I felt, the last child. The butcher's shop and church were seen only under hypnosis. 3

Armed with these memories and dates, Jenny visited Ireland. to search for the fate of her children. She found both the church and the butcher shop and eventually the remnants of the old cottage she had made do with as Mary Sutton. She was able to locate her oldest "son", who took the reunion in stride. Eventually with the help of the BBC all the children were located.

The question that naturally arises, assuming these past life remembrances are valid, do they serve a useful purpose? Would Jenny's life been happier without the past life worries? Was there any benefit to remembering that lifetime? Certainly, it was psychologically distressful. However, the peace that came from finding her children was enormously satisfying: "The best thing about meeting Sonny, apart from getting to know a really lovely person, was finding out at last what had happened to the family after Mary's death. The news about them was by no means good but at least now I knew."3 Apparently only the youngest child, baby Elizabeth was taken in by family and the other the children were eventually removed from the father and placed in orphanages run by Christian charities.

For the millions who do embrace the wisdom of reincarnation, there is great comfort in knowing life continues. Life takes on a greater purpose. Eventually the truth sets us free, as Edgar Cayce explained to a woman who was a teacher in this life, but had been Carpathian princess who studied in the mystery schools of ancient Egypt, and later returned as one known as Judy in Palestine. She was given this advice:" Yet know in the awareness that ye will find more and more the *truth,* which indeed sets one *free.* Not to the convention of the material policies or activities, but in *spirit* and in *truth* !" In the final analysis, it is what is in our hearts or our intentions that count spiritually. In this case, the teacher. and seeker of spiritual truth, she had earned the privilege of" reincarnation unnecessary"-- the highest goal one can attain in this life!

The law of karma becomes the Golden Rule leading us from one life to another It is through what the Hindus call samskaras that become in effect our subconscious desires which guide the next life. These desire can be sensual or spiritual depending on our awareness. Throughout the ages, each person has the potential to be a blessing or a burden to others. With this in mind, it is wise not to take on a study of past lives whether though dreams or past life regression for the reason of self aggrandizement , but rather in the spirit of acquiring healing, guidance, and more spiritual awareness.

With these cautionary notes in mind, what is the best method to gain knowledge of past life remembrance? There are three: spontaneous dreams and astral travel, dream incubation, and guided astral travel. If you wish to have more spontaneous remembrances, then immerse yourself in literature regarding reincarnation. You may also consciously send the thought "I would like view a past life that is help in this life." Then take time to carefully record your dreams. As you build up a body of literature on your past lives, you will receive more and more information from your guides and the akashic records.

End Notes

1. Michael Schmicker, *Best Evidence*, Writer's Club Press, New York, NY page 269.
2. Arthur Guirdham, *The Cathars and Reincarnation*, 1970, C. W. Daniel Publisher, Essex, England, page 11.
3. Jeffrey Furst, The Return of Frances Willard, Pyramid Books, 1973, New York, NY.
4. Jenny Cockell, *Across Time and Death*, 1993, Firestone Books, New York, NY, page 127.

Chapter Twelve:
Akashic Records

Edgar Cayce was particularly adept at not reading the future but also the akashic records. The Sleeping Prophet, loosened his tie and laid down on the couch with his head to the north. While in trance, Edgar Cayce described traveling to a library on the other side and being handed a Book of Life by a brown-robed monk. When asked about the Book of Life, the source said, "Upon time and space is written the thoughts, the deeds, the activities of an entity—as its relationships to its environs, its hereditary influence. as directed or judgment drawn by or according to what the entity's ideal is."1

Edgar Cayce gave 2500 life of these life readings from 1923 to 1945. He often advised his clients that their current issues stemmed from past lives. In one reading, he told Patricia Farrier, a 45 year old woman that her claustrophobia stemmed from a lifetime in Virginia where she been had smothered to death. In that life as Geraldine Fairfax, her colonial farmhouse collapsed, literally smothering the thirteen-year old girl to death.

Cayce obtained his own past life reading. In one life he had been an Egyptian priest, Ra Ta. Cayce reached the zenith of his own spiritual abilities in Egypt; however, he fell from favor by taking a second wife. When Ra Ta broke the law that he himself had decreed concerning the number of wives accorded to or given to the priest, a religious war ensued. Ra Ta and the Princess Isis were banished with all his followers. 2

This triangle came back in the 1900s. Ra Ta returned as the sleeping prophet with the same wives he had in Egypt—his wife Gertrude and secretary Gladys Davis. However, instead of rebelling against the spiritual laws, the three joined forces and brought through the work of Edgar Cayce to the masses. Cayce's guide, the Source, emphasized the importance of reading the akashic records, not so much for self-aggrandizement, but rather, to understand one's short-coming, so the individual could make amends in the present life. In this life, Gladys remained a faithful secretary to Edgar Cayce and a friend to Mrs. Cayce who treated her as a daughter.

Another interesting case involved the return of the noted suffragette, Frances Willard. In 1939, Cayce told two young parents that their baby Patty had lived previously as Frances Willard (1839-1898). The parents wisely kept this information from their daughter until she was sixteen. Even so,. Patty frequently sang Willard's favorite hymn "Rock of Ages" and covered her walls with the same Japanese water-colors that hung in Frances Willard's Oberlin, Ohio home. The list of coincidences went on and on. As a child Patty enjoyed "lecturing" to invisible audience as well as helping others. The physical resemblance between the two was uncanny, as both women were vegetarians and prone to anemia.3 In 1971 author Jeffrey Furst wrote a book on Patty detailing the many similarities that existed between Patty and Frances Willard, titled The Return of Frances Willard.

Edgar Cayce was not alone in his belief in the akashic records. The Hindus, Tibetans, Egyptians, Persians, Chaldeans, Greeks, Chinese, Hebrews, Christians, Druids and Mayans also believed in their existence. In fact the Indian sages of the Himalayas believed that activities of each soul were recorded in a "book" which could be read by mental attunement. Other individuals who claim to have had access to their Akashic Records include: Nostradamus, Charles Webster Leadbeater, Annie Besant, Alice Bailey, William Lilly, Manly P. Hall, Dion Fortune, Rudolf Steiner, Max Heindel, and Jane Roberts.

Jane Roberts wrote in the Seth books that Seth explains "that the fundamental stuff of the universe is ideas and consciousness, and that an idea once conceived exists forever. " Rosicrucian's, Max Heindel calls them 'the memory of Nature' which may be read in three areas of inner consciousness. In the *reflecting ether* of the etheric region there are pictures of all that has happened in the world - at least several hundred years back, or much more in some cases - and they appear almost as the pictures on a screen, with the difference that the scene shifts backward. " 4 Rudolf Steiner in *Cosmic Memory* says. "One who has acquired the ability to perceive the spiritual world comes to know past events and their eternal character. They do not stand before him like the dead testimony of history, but appear in full life."

One way to access your akashic records is through guided imagery. Before you do this exercise, decide on a question or information you would like to receive from your Book of Life known as the Akashic Records Lie or sit in a comfortable position and have a friend read the following hypnosis exercise:

Guided Imagery: Journey to the Akashic Records

Try this hypnosis exercise to relax your body. For best results have someone read it to you. Sit in a comfortable position. Uncross your legs. Now take a deep breath through the nose and out through the mouth.

Do this three times. Relax your eyes.

Take three deep breaths. We all have a book of life on the other side where your akashic records are kept by the Masters. Here, you can look up any question and receive information. Your personal book of life is kept in a library on the other side staffed with religious people such as monks and nuns. It is your privilege to visit this library on the other side.

As you prepare for your journey, ask your guides to be with you.

Pause.

Take three deep breaths. Breathe in peace. Breathe out stress.

Surround yourself with the white light of protection.

Imagine you are looking a pool of aqua water with white lotus blossoms gently skimming the surface.

Relax your eye muscles as you gaze at this beautiful scene.

Allow this feeling of relaxation to go into your forehead erasing any stress, into your cheeks, ears mouth, throat-- your entire face.

You may wish to part your lips a bit just to relax your jaw.

Now this feeling of relaxation is traveling down your neck into your shoulders, releasing all stress.

Feel the relaxation travel down your spine. Your spine is a flexible as a piece of spaghetti--every vertebrae in place.

Next, center the relaxation on your right shoulder and feeling travel down your right shoulder to your right elbow to your right write to your right finger tips Your whole right arm from the shoulder to finger tips is completely relaxed.

Next, center the relaxation on your left shoulder and feeling travel down your left shoulder to your left elbow to your left wrist to your left finger tips Your whole left arm from the shoulder to finger tips is completely relaxed.

Allow the relaxation to enters your chest. Feel your breathing become more rhythmic. It is so easy to breathe in and out.

In and out.

Your heart is beating rhythmically. Soft, gentle beats.

Next center the relaxation on your left hip and feel it travel down your left leg to your left thigh your left ankle to your left foot Your whole left leg from hip socket to the sole of your foot is completely relaxed.

Your whole body is completely at peace, totally relaxed.

Your whole body is completely at peace, totally relaxed.

Breathe deeply in through the nose and out through the mouth.

Focus your attention on your eye.

Allow the area in the midst of your forehead to soften.

Feel the energy expand as you focus on the third eye.

Feel a bright light around your third eye--penetrating and opening it even wider.

Feel a comforting warm pulsation on your forehead.

Allow the light to open your inner vision completely.

Focus this radiant light outward.

See yourself in front of a spiral staircase. On the count of seven you will walk down each of the

seven stairs. When I say seven-- but not before you will be in an old library-- where your book of life is kept. Take your time, put your hand on the railing and feel yourself going down seven stairs.

One, release any tension.

Two.

Three down, down, down.

Four.

Five. Almost there.

Six.

And seven, you are know in the library.

As you look around you can see a monk who is filled with compassion and wisdom. The library is quiet, a holy place of peace and calm. The monk goes to the book shelf and selects your Book of Life and places it on a table before you.. You feel excited and happy . These are the Akashic Records where the wisdom of all your lives is kept. In a moment as I say the number three you will open the book and find the answer to your question. Ask your question now.

Put your hands on the book

One.

Two.

Three.

Open to the page which has the answer to your question.

As you open the book, you are astounded by the wisdom

Take a moment to see or sense the answer.

Enjoy the book. Take a few minutes while you read the passages you need to give your guidance and transform your thinking .

(Play soft music for three to five minutes)

Very good.

You will remember all the details. Thank your guide.

Now you are ready to return . See yourself at the bottom of the staircase. In your mind's eye, begin walking back up the stairs. One step at a time. As I say each number, you will go up one step until I say seven when you will be back to where you began the session.

One. You are ready to return.

Two. You feel rested.

Three. You feel wonderful in every way.

Four You have peace of mind.

Five You are waking up.

Six You are ready to come back.

Seven-- eyes wide awake.

Write your impressions down immediately. Later, review your notes. Often you will be surprised at how accurate the information is!

Chapter Thirteen:
Famous and Infamous Prophets

When the iron eagle flies and horses run on wheels, the Tibetan people will be scattered over the earth, and the dharma *will go to the land of the Red Man (the West).* **Padmasambhava** *8th century AD*

The ancients were well versed in the mystical arts of astral travel, visions, and prophecy. In India, for instance, the 8th Century prophet, Padmasambhava, is considered a second Buddha. He foresaw the current age of air planes and cars. He also saw " It is even stranger that people in that era do not need to leave their houses to know things that happen around the world, just by sitting in front of a mirror.1 Apparently the prophet, Padmasambhava, was even able to foresee television.

In the West, Plato considered prophesy the noblest of arts. Socrates termed it "Divine Madness". Even the Bible recognizes prophets "We have also a more sure word of prophecy where unto ye do well that ye take heed, as unto a light that shineth in a dark place, until the day dawn, and the day star arise in your hearts."1. However, in the Book of Mathew, Jesus warns "Watch out for false prophets. They come to you in sheep's clothing, but inwardly they are ferocious wolves."

Why the divergent views? It is because prophets, as with psychics and mediums vary in their talents. Some are genuinely inspired from on high, while others are motivated by lower forces of greed and ego. Also, many genuinely gifted prophets can be off in their timing due to free will. For example, Edgar Cayce explained when an earth quake which had been predicted for the San Francisco area in the 1930s did not occur, it was due to the cooperation and good will of those who built the Golden Gate Bridge.

Gordon Michael Scallion is an example of a modern prophet who though often accurate can be off in his timing. Originally, he believed earth changes would occur by 2002, but then he pushed the date farther ahead. He still believes "The whole planet is heating up and going through a 'metamorphosis' that is triggered by magnetic shifts and movements in the Earth's core."1 The author of Earth Change Reports admits "We need to see whatever happens as a cycle that the earth is going through. The outcome has not been determined".2

Biblical prophets seem to be very aware of free will. The prophets of the Old Testament were the watchmen of God. Their sacred task was to communicate God's will to man. The four major Biblical prophets--Isaiah, Jeremiah, Ezekiel, and Daniel all used different methods to divine God's will; they were, however, all concerned with helping the Jews of Judea. For instance,

In Isaiah, God promised "If ye will be my people, I will be your God." Isaiah (740-680 B.C.) also warned the Jew against forming alliances with foreign powers of Assyria and Egypt.. " The Lord had told him such actions would lead to ruin for the Jews of Judea. However people have free will and chose to follow their political leader rather than the word of God."4

The next major prophet, Jeremiah,627-585 B.C. was a contemporary of Daniel and Ezekiel. He warn against idolatry and chastised the people of Judah for the sacrifice of their children to foreign places. However, Jeremiah give hope if the Jews will repent. The two major themes in the book are warning people of God's judgment could even involve the sacrifice of their children to foreign gods. Jeremiah also reminds his people of their sacred covenant with God "But this is what I commanded them, saying, 'Obey My voice, and I will be your God, and you will be My people; and you will walk in all the way which I command you, that it may be well with you." 5 Those who do not obey, will go backward.

Ezekiel likewise talks of a savior who has the right to rule and who will minister as the true Shepherd..One of the most vivid vision is that of :God or Yahweh approaching Ezekiel as the divine warrior. and an eagle), and four wings.6 The same images are present on the great Sphinx and thought to be the astrological signs of Taurus, Leo, Scorpio and Aquarius. Each creature is a is a "wheel within a wheel," God commission Ezekiel as his prophet "Son of man, I am sending you to the Israelites. 7 Some New Age scholars feel these "chariots of fire" could be a reference to UFOs.

Many Biblical characters have had supernatural events including Jesus, Peter, James, John, and Paul in the New Testament and Enoch, Moses, Aaron, Abraham and Daniel in the Old Testament In fact, an extraordinary occurrence played a role in the life of the prophet Daniel-- specifically when a disembodied fingers write on the wall of the royal palace. When King Belshazzar asked Daniel to interpret the writing and Daniel gives this warning: "And this is the writing that was inscribed: *mina*, *mina*, *shekel*, *half-mina*. This is the interpretation of the matter: *mina*, God has numbered the days of your kingdom and brought it to an end; *shekel*, you have been weighed on the scales and found wanting; *half-mina*, your kingdom is divided and given to the Medes and Persians.7 That very night King Belshazzar is murdered and Darius the Mede is made king.

Later-day prophets also used their extra sensory perception to obtain their information. Michel de Nostredame (1503- 1566), for instance, used scrying. Nostradamus is best known for his book *Les Propheties*, which first appeared in 1555. Most of the passages deal with wars, floods, invasions and murders. One theme is that of the invasion of Europe by Muslins headed by the third of three anti-Christs. Nostradamus scholars have pegged Napoleon as the first anti-Christ, followed by Hitler and a third yet to be revealed.

Edgar Cayce, whom many considered a second Nostradamus, used trance to obtain information. A prolific channeler, Edgar Cayce gave over 14,000 readings during from 1901 to 1944. He soon became known for medical readings. However, he expanded to topics such as meditation, dreams, reincarnation, and prophecy due to the influence of Arthur Lammers, a wealthy printer and student of metaphysics. 1923 Cayce gave Lammers readings on past lives, astrology, and mysticism. Cayce also discussed Universal law:- "As ye judge, so shall ye be judged." Cayce guides also explained that God has promised to guide his people on their spiritual path.

For the most part, Cayce was a very accurate prophet. He is on record as having predicted the stock market crash of 1929, World War II, and the use of a drop of blood to diagnose the body. He described the Essenes well before the Dead Sea Sculls surfaced in 1947. He also foresaw his own death at age 69. Some of Cayce's prophecies have yet to come to pass. For instance in 1926, he predicted "gasless motor" which has yet to appear on the market-- unless he was referring to the use of electricity to run cars. He also predicted that records form Atlantis would be found brined underneath the sphinx. As to the future of nations, Cayce predicted China would become "the cradle of Christianity." 8 Last but not least, in a July 9, 1933 session

Edgar Cayce said that there would be a second coming as promised by the prophets of old "in this day and generation, and that soon there will again appear in the earth that one through whom many will be called to meet those that are preparing the way for His day in the earth. The Lord, then, will come, 'even as ye have seen him go."19

While there have been many famous prophets, there have also been a few infamous. Sadly, many people follow blindly such as the Branch Dravidians who believed the self-proclaimed prophet David Koresh and the People's Temple members who fell under the spell of Rev. Jim Jones. False prophets are not new . Perhaps the most famous of the false prophets was William Miller He began to preach about the end of world in the 1840s, stating that Jesus Christ would return and that Earth would go up in flames between March 21, 1843, and March 21, 1844. As many as 100,000 "Millerites" sold their possessions between 1840 and 1844 and waited in the mountain for the world to end. Most of followers left the movement disillusioned; however a few stuck by Miller and went on to form the Seventh-day Adventist movement. If only the followers of David Koresh and Jim Jones had to experience their loss of faith-- instead of losing their lives to the dictates of false prophets.

End Notes

1. Holy Bible, Peter 1:19.
2.http://thevictoryreport.org/2012/11/23/gordon-michael-scallion-earth-changes-america/
3. http://www.crystalinks.com/gms.html.
4. Holy Bible, Isaiah, 11:1.
5. Holy Bible, Jeremiah 7:23-24.
6. Holy Bible Ezekiel 1:1-3:27.
7. Holy Bible, Daniel 5:25-28.
8 Edgar Cayce, Reading 3976-29.
9. Edgar Cayce, Reading 262-49.

Chapter Fourteen:
Prophetic Dreams

Through his own dreams, a person may gain more understanding of those forces that go to make the real existence—what it's all about and what it's good for—if the individual would but comprehend the conditions being manifested. **Edgar Cayce**

One of the more reliable forms of prophecy is dreams. For more than three thousand years ago, Egyptians believed that they could contact the gods in their dreams and that these dreams served as oracle. The ancient Egyptians would even go out of their way to visit famous temples such as the temple at Memphis. Here they would sleep in the hope of reviewing a dream revelation

The Greeks also believed in dream incubation and insisted on purification before interring the temple: "Two days before entering the shrine (Shrine of Apollo at Delphi) they abstained from sex, ate no meat, fish or fowl, and drank only water. In addition an animal sacrifice was made to the god whom they wished to invoke through a dream." 1 Then the dream would sleep in the skin of the sacrificed animal in the hopes of contacting to contact the God of Healing Ascepelius."

Hippocrates in particular believed that both mind and body were important in healing and believed that dreams could be of assistance eon booth diagnosis and treatment Years before. Sigmund Freud, Hippocrates was one of the first physicians who tried to provide a scientific account of dreams. "Hippocrates was even able to postulate that dreams were indicators of psychic problems. A dream about eating, for example, meant that the dreamer was suffering from depression and was trying to make up for some deficiency. Two thousand years later, Dr. Sigmund Freud would interpret a dream of this nature the same way, call the dream an example of "compensation." 2

The ancient Hebrews who believed in one God, incubated dreams in order to receive help from the Divine. For instance, the Hebrew prophet Samuel slept in the in the temple at Shiloh to receive the word of God. The Bible details Jacob's dream of climbing on a ladder and ascended to heaven. In Jacob's prophetic dream, God promised Jacob that Israel would remain the property of the Jewish people/.In the New Testament Joseph was told in a dream about Herod edict, so they fled with baby Jesus into Egypt.

Another dramatic warning in dream went unheeded. Henry III of France had this prophetic dream just days before his assassination "Three days before his assassination in 1589 by Jacques Clement, a monk, he dreamed that all the royal vestments, royal tunics, and the orb and scepter were bloodied and trampled underfoot by monks. Later his successor, Henry IIV dreamed of a rainbow over his head, a sign of a violent death the night before his assassination by Francois Ravaillac. 3

Bishop Joseph Lenyi of Grosswardein, also had a vivid assassination dream. The Bishop, who had been a tutor of the Archduke Duke Franz Ferdinand of Austria was awakened at quarter of four in the morning by a disturbing dream in which saw a picture of two men assassinate the archduke and his wife. He even saw a black- bordered letter with the official coat of arms of the archduke. The note read as follows:

Dear Dr. Lanyi,
I hereby inform you that tomorrow, my wife and I will fall victims to assassination. We commend ourselves to your pious prayers.

Kindest regards from
Archduke Franz
Sarajevo, the 28th of June 3:48 A.M.

The Bishop even drew a picture of the narrow street and motor car at the scene of the murder which was exact save one detail, there was only one assassin.4

Psychologists also have had their share of prophetic dreams. For instance, psychologist, Dr. Carl Jung believed in the power of dreams to foretell the future. He frequently was able to tune into what he termed the Collective Unconscious. In one of his visions, he saw a huge flood cover Europe with bodies floating in muddy water which turned to blood. One year, later August of 1914, World War I broke out.

Jungian psychologists such as James Kirsch have great respect for dreams. He wrote a book on the prophetic dreams of Orthodox Jewish rabbi, Hyle Wechsler. In 1881, wrote a pamphlet entitled A Word of Warning which detailed a series of dreams he had of future genocide of Jews in western Europe. Tragically, Rabbi Wechsler dire prophecy came true sixty years later with Hitler's concentration camps of World War II.5

Many people reported vivid dreams preceding the 9/11 attack on the twin towers. The Boundary Institute, for example, received many report of prophetic 9/11 dreams. such as the following: vivid dream occurred a few days before the attack: "One woman reported a dream in which she saw herself running down a city street. She said "I was passing parked cars and I could hear people all around me screaming as they ran along with me. I looked back and I could see the debris and dust cloud gaining on me and I thought that if I ditched under one of the parked cars that I could somehow avoid getting hit by the larger stuff that was being carried along in the cloud. I covered my face once under a car and remember feeling like I was choking". 6

For most dreamers precognitive dreams may take the form of seeing someone in a rheas before you meet them for the first time or more mundane events such as dreaming about visiting a friend and then later finding the meeting to be exactly as you saw it in the dream. One dreamer reported visiting her friend, Paula, in Paula's bedroom. For some odd reason, the dreamer was with her husband who never visited Paula. In the dream, the three were deep in conversation. At the time the dream did not make any sense but it stayed with her. About four months later, she went to pick up a buffet that she bought from Paula and asked her husband to come with her to put the buffet in their van. While they were picking up the buffet, Paula asked the couple if they be interested in a chair which was in her bedroom. They then went upstairs to look at the chair which the dreamer decided against. However they began an animated conversation just like in the dream!

How can such things happen According to the Tibetans, it is possible to see the future by traveling the time lines. "In Tibetan Buddhism, it is said that the inner mind or Kunshi, 'base of the mind', records all the memories of past and present experiences of the body and mind. The reflections of the memory - that is released or moved by similar experiences that the person earned or will earn in the day or next days may appear in the dream as premonitory or through dreams, the inner world of the body/mind."7 The Bon sect have particular faith in dreams They utilize to contact spirit of the dead, diagnose diseases and even make about politics of the nation.

Westerners also record dreams visitation from the dead. One dreamer, Ellie, a middle aged woman dreamed of her grandfather. The dream was so real that she could feel the bones in his hand when she clutched hand of her deceased grandfather. Ellie was just about to wake her husband to ask if the grandfather could come and live with them when she remember that he had died twenty years ago! This type of dream would be termed an apparition.

Warning dreams and visits from the deceased are common in dreams, but so is dream telepathy in which two people meet in a dreams often to discuss or solve an issue. One poignant example comes to mind. Dorothy had a disagreement with her friend, Molly who was usually most kind and gracious. With the passage of time, Dorothy let the matter go. Sadly, Molly passed away a few years later from lung cancer. After Molly's passing, Dorothy had a dream in which Molly gave Dorothy a heart-felt hug. When she woke up Dorothy was at peace The message was "We are friends again."

Other warning dreams may prepare one for disaster. One such dream occurred in April 29, 1929. The dreamer was a Wall Street broker and client of Edgar Cayce's. The dreamer discussed this dream with the famous psychic over the phone:"Dreamed we should sell all our stocks including box stock [one considered very good]. I saw a bull following my wife, who was dressed in red."Cayce interpreted the dream to indicate a downward turn in the market and urged the successful stockbroker to dispose of his stock holdings even those that he considered safe as a great change was coming.:

While some dreams warn the dreamers of danger, others prepare them for impending tragedy. For instance, Barbara, a 40 year old real estate agent an mother of two teen aged boys had a dream in which she was cleaning out the glove compartment of her 16 year old's car. A week later, her son was killed in a car accident on his way to work. She completely forgot the dream until a month later, when she was cleaning out his glove compartment just like in her dream. "In a strange way , it gave me comfort. It was as if he was destined for a short life." A medium later confirm that her son had signed for a short life and at peace on the other side.

Sometimes dreams can be a buffer against negative energy. Judy, a psychic medium, had a dream in which a fifty year old woman came in and pointed out the butterflies on the wall paper that graced her dining room wall. Then the client came into her office and sat down for a reading. At the end of the session, she said to the medium, "I don't believe in this at all." Of course, Judy was surprised by the comment. When she awoke, she was puzzled by her dream. However, the mystery was solved three months when a middle-age woman came for a session. After the reading, she handed Judy her fee and said, "I don't really believe in this." She felt a twinge of pain. However, when her client stopped to admire the butterflies on the dining room wall paper, at that moment, Judy remembered her dream three months before and felt as if it was all meant to be. Instead of feeling hurt, the veteran medium just shrugged.

Prophetic dreams can be spontaneous gifts from the other side. According to Hindu interpretation, dreams are genuine and often come from higher world. This type of dream may be invoked through conscious efforts of meditation, prayers, and charity. Other dreams according to Hindu text such as *Charaka-Samhita* by Charaka are due to retribution of the dreamer's thoughts and actions. For instance, a pure heart attracts happy dreams, while ill intentions brings sorrowful dreams. In extreme cases, a dissolute life style can also attract evil spirits.

Dreams,. after all, are an interactive process. For those who wish to increase the probably of a prophetic dreams, it is important to use the power of prayer, intention and extra time in the dream state. Start with a long baths to wash away the cares (and the vibrations) of the day. It is ok to have a light meal or a glass of milk, but only an hour before bed as a heavy meal can interfere with sleep. Also do not drink alcohol or take drugs, as they infer with REM or dream sleep. Maintain a regular routine to calm the body.

Next work on calming the mind. Our last waking thoughts have a definite effect on dream time. Avoid the news and violent or sensational programs. Instead choose some light reading or better yet one of the dream books listed at the end of the chapter. As you focus more on the spiritual side of life you will draw in positive guidance.

Finally, yourself a suggestion before turning in. Write the suggestion on an index card and place under you p[pillow. try to be as specific as possible . A good request ion make be for informant on the future outcome. For example, "Will my son, Bob be successful if he opens a car wash in Buffalo?" or "If I retire in five what will my future be like?"

Next completely release any expectation. Allow your guides to do the work. If you are ready for the information, they will being it though. If no prophetic dreams occurs, do some spiritual work or charity and try again in a month. After three attempts, allow the matter to rest. It may be, it is not the right time to receive the answer. Have faith, that when you are ready, the answer will appear in a dream.

End Notes

1. http://library.thinkquest.org/26857/historyofdreams.httm.
2. http://www.examiner.com/article/significance-of-dreams-according-to-ancient-civilizations.
3. Our Dreaming Mind, Robert Van De Castle, Random House, New York, NY 1994, page 28.
4. Our Dreaming Mind, Robert Van De Castle, Random House, New York, NY 1994, page 28-29.
5. Our Dreaming Mind, Robert Van De Castle, Random House, New York, NY 1994, page 28-29.
6. http://www.boundaryinstitute.org/bi/premon911.htm.
7. http://www.tibetanmedicine-edu.org/index.php/dream-practice.

Chapter Fifteen:
Dreaming True

I slept and dreamed that life was joy.
I woke, and found that life was service.
I acted, and found that service was joy. **Rabindranath Tagore**

In his book, *Dreams That Come True,* Dr. David Ryback described how he became a believer in dreaming true when a survey of his college students revealed that 65 percent of them had had precognitive dreams. "When half of the class provided examples, his rigorous analytic criteria found that eight percent of the class had dream experiences that suggested paranormal future-sensing as the most likely explanation." After further analysis, the psychologist came to the conclusion about one in twelve people have "evidentiary precognitive dreams." 1

Another researcher, Dr. Luisa Rhine, would have agreed with Dr. Ryback. She collected over 7,000 possible precognitive dreams, of which 433 detailed events that might have been altered had the dreamer taken action. Fifty percent of these dreams involved death. Women were twice as likely to be recipients of precognitive dreams, and most precognitive dreams involved blood relative, spouses and close friends." 2 Apparently some personal tie helps to activate the dream.

Unfortunately prophetic dreams are not always reliable Sometimes the time is off, and other times free will may change the prediction. For instance while Bishop Joseph Lenyi had many details correct in his dream of Archduke Franz, however he was wrong on the number of assassins. . Could it be that one of the assassins backed out at the last moment?

Perhaps Bishop Joseph Lenyi's ardent prayers caused the change in plans. When the priest dreamt his former student the Archduke was in danger, .he immediately started to pray the rosary, and later called on his mother and a guest to join him to offer a high mass for the Archduke Franz Ferdinand.1 However, the bishop was not able to warn his beloved pupil. Had he been able to do so, the bishop may have been able to stop the assassination of Franz Ferdinand which set off World War I.

Knowledge gleaned from dreams has great potential to help humanity, yet few psychologists take paranormal dreams take paranormal dreams seriously. They are simply not trained in parapsychology. Those who do such as Dr. Joseph B. Rhine, Dr. Luisa Rhine, Dr. Calvin Hall Dr. Montague Ullman, Dr. Scott Sparrow, and Dr. Dean Radin are often ignored by their colleagues.

What can be done to remedy the situation? First, more scientific study of dreams is necessary. Now that science has concluded that everyone dreams one and half to two hours every night, perhaps it is ready to tackle the question of why people dream. Is it just wish fulfillment as explained by Dr. Sigmund Freud or does the dreamer delve into the world of the collective unconscious as postulated by Dr. Carl Jung? Could dreams be the result of dream telepathy as shown in the studied conducted by Dr. Montague Ullman? Could the dreamer be having paranormal experiences of the lucid dream state studied by Dr. Scott Sparrow?

Dr Dean Radin has come with some very intriguing information. Radin (born February 29, 1952) is the author of Conscious Universe Entangled Minds. This respected researcher in parapsychology, states " Psi has been shown to exist in thousands of experiments. There are disagreements over to how to interpret the evidence, but the fact is that virtually all scientists who have studied the evidence, including the hard-nosed skeptics, now agree that there is something interesting going on that merits serious scientific attention." 3

For the record, parapsychologists have studied clairvoyance, telepathy, psycho kinesis and prophecy for over a century. Only recently has science ventured into studies of reincarnation through the research efforts of psychiatrist Dr. Ian T. Stevenson who collected 3,000 case studies of children from Africa to Alaska. Remi Cadoret wrote in the *American Journal of Psychiatry* that "typically the children would start talking about past-life memories (and often violent deaths) at the age of two to four, and would stop by the age of eight. The descriptions would be accompanied by unusual behavior such as phobias, and the children might have a birthmark or birth defect the same shape as wounds on the body of the deceased person whose life was purportedly being recalled. 4 Dreams if properly analyzed could be a rich source of information on past lives.

Dreams can also provide legitimate contact with the deceased. In 2008, Dr. Gary Schwartz launched his VERITAS research project, to test the hypothesis that the consciousness (or identity) of a person survives physical death. He performed experiments at the University of Arizona with noted medium, John Edward of TV's Crossing Over and Allison DuBois, the inspiration for the TV drama Medium., Schwartz concluded that medium Alison DuBois could indeed contact dead people, saying, "There is no question this is not a fraud, some people really can do this, and Allison is one of them." Schwartz says his experiments with DuBois included a reading for celebrity physician and author Dr. Deepak Chopra following the death of his father that Chopra characterized as 77% accurate." 5

Where will science take us next? Dr. Raymond Moody, author of Life After Life, has constructed a psychomanteum similar to a chamber used at the Temple of Delphi to communicate with the deceased. Perhaps one day grief counselors will prescribe a reunion with departed loved one either through a medium or a visit to a psychomanteum to ease the pain of bereavement.

Hopefully, the day will come when dreams will be understood for the their vast capacity to contact past, present, and future. For those who wish to do so, here are some suggestions for dreaming true: First realize that dreams are valid. Trust your instincts, but also take time to check the facts. Try to get a clear understanding of what the dream is trying to tell you. Remember a dream is a message from yourself to yourself.

Be willing to take into account past-life remembrances. Some dreams may take you back to a previous life. Many people experience déjà vu in a dream as they visit places they have lived in previous lives. Often these dreams are activated by an event that needs to be resolved in the present life. If you are back in Rome at the time of the persecution of the Christians, it may be that you lived doing that period. Now, you are given the opportunity to assist those you were helpless to save in that life. If you are interested in reincarnation, you will receive more information. Remember to use the information for soul growth-- not self aggrandizement.

Next, take dreams of deceased loved one seriously. This may be their only way of communicating with you. It is a natural to wonder how your loved ones are doing on the other side and it is just as natural for them to be concerned about you. Such communication can be of help to both parties-- as long as it does not become an obsession. Life, after all, is for the living.

When you go to sleep at night, try to be in a relaxed and positive state of mind. Be clear on your intention. Send the thought out before you turn off the lights, "What do I need you know?" Then have faith that a Higher Intelligence can give you information beyond the scope of the human mind through dreams. Sometime this information will come through directly, other times careful interpretation is needed. You will earn the respect of the keepers of the akashic record by your willingness to do your part.

Next, look for precognitive elements in dreams. Often this is shown as being a spectator in a movie theater, watching or reading the news. Some dreamers are taken to a future location through astral travel. Make note of your surroundings. Pay special attention to markers and dates that are presented in dreams.

Finally, utilize the information given. Many a dream has inspired a poem, song or story. Dreams have also been a rich source of knowledge for the inventor and shamans the world over have used dreams for healing. Prophetic dreams are given to help us safely navigate life. Last, but not least, dreaming true can lead to living true.

End Notes

1. *Lucid Dreaming*, Robert Waggoner, Moment Point Press, Needham MA,2009, p 185.
2. *Our Dreaming Mind*, Robert Van De Castle, Random House, New York, NY 1994, page 29.
3. http://www.deanradin.com/NewWeb/deanradin.html.
4. http://en.wikipedia.org/wiki/Ian_Stevenson.
5. http://en.wikipedia.org/wiki/Gary_Schwartz.

Chapter Sixteen:
Have a Good Night!

Yesterday is but today's memory, tomorrow is today's dream. **Kahlil Gibran**

Sleep has not always been viewed as beneficial. During the Middle Ages, people believed sleep was the playground for the devil. It was whispered that a sound sleeper could be under Satanic attack. In order to protect themselves, someone had to keep a vigil during the night so the devil would not cause harm to the sleeper. Of course, a psychologist would say it is the subconscious mind and not the devil that keeps the person awake. During sleep the conscious mind is put aside and the unconscious mind is in charge. Hence fears and anxieties came take over. Frequently, sleepers report nightmares and restless fears as a result. .No wonder, even today, some people are light sleepers!

Preparation for a good night's sleep begins with relaxation. A clear and positive mind can do much to create a restful night, but how does one achieve this? One way to deal with anxiety is through mindfulness. Increasingly, mindfulness is being utilized in Western psychology to alleviate a variety of mental conditions. Mindfulness can be achieved by counting sheep, meditating on a mandala or focusing on the breath, or mindfulness can begin with a simple five minute practice each day. Sit in a comfortable positive in a chair on crossed-leg on prayer mat on the floor. Then close your eyes and focus on your breath. Just feel the breath in and out. If thought intrude your meditation, just go back to focusing on your breath. By noticing and focusing on the breath, the meditation slows down the mind and its mental chatter. Make it a practice to set aside at least five minutes every day to focus on the breath. Soon you will achieve what Buddhist call "right mind."

Science has recently studied the effects of meditation. According to researchers at Brown University "Mindfulness may be so successful in helping with a range of conditions, from depression to pain, by working as a sort of 'volume knob' for sensations"1 Other research published in the *Journal Frontiers in Human Neuroscience* proposed that mindfulness meditation helps people to gain better control over of pain and emotions.

"Specifically, the researchers postulate that mindfulness meditation plays a role in the controlling of cortical alpha rhythms, which have been shown in brain imaging studies to play a role in what senses our bodies and minds pay attention to." 2

Meditation has long been used a means of clearing the mind for sleep. For example, Austrian occultist, Rudolf Steiner (1861–1925) suggested meditation before turning in at night. The founder of the anthroposophy movement advised his student to take a few minutes to review thought and actions as if they were those of another individual. In doing so our own reaction become clear and a object for contemplation For the evening meditation Steiner suggested a reverse meditation . Meditate on the last event before bed and go through to the first of morning Steiner felt by reviewing event in reverse order, it would help to d see things in a new light and help to clear the mind.

Affirmations are also an effective way to clear the mind. The practice was popularized in the 1920s by French pharmacist and psychologist Dr. Emil Coué (1857 –1926) Coué's most popular affirmation was "Every day in every way I am getting better and better. "While he believed in the effects of medication, also felt the patient mental states could affect the medicine as well. an instrument that we possess at birth, and with which we play unconsciously all our life, as a baby plays with its rattle. It is however a dangerous instrument; it can wound or even kill you if you handle it imprudently and unconsciously. It can on the contrary save your life when you know how to employ it consciously."3 He had his patients practice a positive affirmation to replace negative feelings of "thought of illness" with a new "thought of cure". According to Coué, by recitation of auto-suggestion , the subconscious mind can absorbed them. repeating words or images enough times causes the subconscious to can take them in. Dr. Coue claimed that his patients were cured of all kinds of illnesses including kidney problems, diabetes, memory loss, stammering, weakness, atrophy and all sorts of physical and mental illnesses.4

Here are seven affirmation for a restful night's sleep:

A mighty God force goes before me making easy , instant, and perfect my sleep."

I am protected at all times asleep and awake.

I call on Loved Ones, guides and angels to be present in my dreams.

Sleep is a state of relaxation- filled with peaceful dreams.

Silence is powerful. Silence is healing, Silence is wisdom."

I am bathed in God's loving protection. Only good can come my way.

Divine Order prevails in my dreams.

In addition to affirmations, spiritual pictures, crosses and dream catcher can aid sleep. Many Christians sleep better with a cross or crucifix over their beds. A Jew may benefit from the Star of David in the bedroom. Spiritual pictures of Jesus, Mother Mary, Buddha, saints or healers can also be effective. When you travel , bring a travel alter with sacred pictures.

The American Indian made use of a "Dream Catcher" to ward off evil dreams. A dream catcher. is a device made from a willow hoop, on which is woven a loose net or web. The net is then is decorated with personal and sacred items such as feathers and beads. Used properly dream catcher can change the owner's dreams. According to Konrad J. Kaweczynski, "Only good dreams would be al-lowed to filter through… Bad dreams would stay in the net, disappearing with the light of day." 5

Children often benefit from dream catchers, as well as regular routines. If your child suffers from poor sleep. Explain what a dream catcher and ask if they would like one. Then take your youngster to a store and let the child pick out one to go over his or her bed. Make sure your child as a regular time and routine for bedtime. For example, bath, bedtime story, night light and soft music. Adults, by the way also benefit from a regular bedtime routine.

Another excellent sleep aid is a white noise machine. White noise is a combination of the many frequencies of sound. that can help fall asleep. It can also help cover up disturbing sounds such as a noisy street or neighbor. Who can benefit from the use of a white noise machine. Studies show intensive-care unit patient sleep netter as do those with intense anxiety disorder such as Post traumatic stress disorder. It also can help night-shift who must sleep during the day. White noise may even help babies fall asleep. White noise machines recommended for babies and young adults have been formulated with the sound of the mother's heartbeat, the sound a cascading waterfall, sounds heard in the womb, and even the peaceful sounds of dolphins at play.

In conclusion, there are many means to achieve a good night's sleep. Here is a summary of the most common suggestions for a good night's sleep:

1. Crate a restful space for sleep. Your bedroom should be a private oasis. Make sure it is clean and well ventilated. Put up light blocking curtains. If possible install an air purifier or humidifier to improve air quality. Add a night light for safety and if desired a white noise machine. Decorate the bedroom with calm, cool colors such as light turquoise or ,sage green. Remove the TV. and computer from your bedroom. Last but not least organize your bedroom and keep clothing and other personal items where they belong.

2. Now that you have calm environment for sleep, use it..Sleep only in your bedroom. If you cannot go to sleep, do not stay in your bed. Go to another part of the house and try a distraction such a watching TV or reading a book.

3. Avoid violent novels or disturbing TV show before bedtime.

4. Establish a regular routine such as a relaxing bath before turning in. You can add lavender scent to increase relaxation. Put on night clothes made of fresh cotton that are loose in fit.

5. Choose a light or spiritual book to read before bed.

6. Try a brief meditation

7. Say an affirmation or prayer.

Have a good night!

Suggested Reading

Dr. Douglas Baker	**Practical Techniques of Astral Projection**
H. F. Provost Battersby	**Man Outside Himself**
Harmon Hartzel Bro	**Edgar Cayce on Dreams,**
William Buhlman	**Adventures Beyond the Body**
Earlyne Chaney	**Initiation in the Great Pyramid,**
Eileen J. Garrett	**Awareness**
Craig Hamilton-Parker	**Remembering Your Dreams**
Sidney Kirkpatrick	**Edgar Cayce: An American Prophet**
Elaine Kuzmeskus	**The Art of Mediumship**
Stephen Leberge,	**Exploring the Lucid Power of Dreams**
Joseph McMoneagle	**The Ultimate Time Machine**
Robert Moss	**Dream Gates**
	Secret History of Dreaming
	The Dreamers Book of the Dead
Robert Monroe	**Journey Out of Body**
A. E. Powell	**The Astral Body**
Scott Rogo	**Leaving the Body**
	Our Psychic Potentials
Jess Stearn	**The Sleeping Prophet**
Elsie Sechrist,	**Dreams: Your Magic Mirror**
	Meditation: Gateway to
Light	
Ed Tick	**The Practice of Dream Healing**
Kevin Todeschi	**Dream Images and Symbols**
Robert Van De Castle	**Our Dreaming Mind,**
Dr. Waldo Vieira	**Projections of the Consciousness**
Richard Webster	**Astral Travel for Beginners**
Paramahansa Yogananda	**Autobiography of a Yogi**

Books by Elaine M. Kuzmeskus

Soul Cycles: Astrology 101
Connecticut Ghosts
Seance 101: Physical Mediumship
The Making of a Medium (autobiography)
The Art of Mediumship

To purchase books, go to author's web site:
www.theartofmediumship.com

CPSIA information can be obtained
at www.ICGtesting.com
Printed in the USA
FFHW012236300719
53958721-59670FF